Your Path to Publication

Your Path to Publication

A Guide to Navigating the World of Publishing

Kim Wright

Press 53
Winston-Salem

Press 53
PO Box 30314
Winston-Salem, NC 27130
www.Press53.com

First Edition

Cover design by Kevin Morgan Watson

Cover art licensed through iStockphoto

Library of Congress Control Number: 2011914805

Printed on acid-free paper
ISBN 978-1-935708-42-1

Contents

Introduction

Just after I sold my first novel, I was at an artist colony in New England where I found myself in conversation with two other writers who had also just sold their first novels...

Wait a minute. Eighty-six that sentence. It's snooty and obnoxious and, worst of all, it plays into the most dangerous myth of the creative life — i.e. that it's glamorous and easy. The truth of the matter is that, yeah, I'd sold my book, but it had taken me eight years to write it, three more to find an agent, and then the publisher sat on the manuscript for two more years. On that Melville-esque November afternoon in question, I was in a gloomy state of mind. This novel had been the chief obsession of my life between the ages of thirty-nine and fifty-two and I still had no idea if this project would ever pay off in any measurable sense.

So I wasn't feeling exactly confident on that dark afternoon, but at least the setting was perfect and we all more or less looked the part. Bill, a retired professor in his seventies, had a gray beard and a plaid shirt. Helena, a hipster memoirist from Brooklyn, was heavily tattooed and her pouty lips turned down into the perpetually sullen expression of a young intellectual. I always wear black — more because I'm pudgy than because I'm arty — so I assume that I was wearing black that day, and furthermore, I'd say it's a safe bet that my expression was tortured. We had the wine, the fire, the costumes, and we even had the book deals.

What we didn't have was the slightest clue about what came next. Or even if the feelings we were all experiencing were normal and survivable.

There are plenty of books about writing, and many of them are excellent. But there's nowhere near as much information on what happens after the writing — navigating the experience of publishing and all that comes with it. That's what this book is — an exploration of the things I wish I'd known on that rainy afternoon three years ago.

Bill and Helena were, like me, somewhere in that limbo state between the time a book has sold and when it comes out. This long period of waiting, waiting, waiting — as I said, for me it went on for more than two years — is enough to turn even a well-adjusted person into a basket case. The chance to converse with other debut novelists — people who could perhaps identify with what I was going through and weren't likely to say something well-intentioned, but stupid — was a rare treat. Writers work in isolation. They're sometimes physically and almost always psychologically removed from the industry that publishes their books. Unless we consciously create these opportunities, we can go years without meeting people in the same line of work, much less people who are at the same point in the process. We rarely have the chance to learn from each other, swap war stories, or confess our doubts and fears to someone who knows first-hand how confusing the publication process can be. Through no fault of their own, my friends and family had no concept of what I was going through, the exhilarating and nauseating swirl of emotions that erupt when you're just on the verge of getting what you always said you wanted. These people on the couch with me… I figured they would understand.

Beyond the surface similarity of being writers who'd sold their first books and were at the colony to work on their second, the three of us would have seemed to have very little in common. I was a Southerner in my early fifties, with a background in non-fiction, who for years had made her living as a food, wine, and travel writer. Bill was in his seventies, living in a small town in Montana in a cabin he had built himself from a kit. Helena was in her late twenties, Ivy League-educated and determined to prove there was more to her than Daddy's money and a Betty Boop face. But none of that seemed to matter. We were so delighted to have found each other that we'd practically fallen into each other's arms with relief. Despite having nearly a hundred years of writing experience among us, the best analogy we'd been able to come up with was that we were all in the same boat.

But pretty soon into the conversation it became clear that, same boat or not, we were on completely different voyages.

Bill was being published by a university press, a small operation that had allowed him to have almost complete control over his process. He'd been edited very lightly and had been consulted about the book's cover and a slight change in title. Whereas most novelists are painfully aware they have a small window of time to establish a readership before their books are shipped back from booksellers and — fearful word! — "remaindered," the university press had promised Bill they would keep his novel in print and available for years. He felt confident this was true; his publisher maintained a huge backlist, meaning that even books published thirty years earlier were still available to readers who wanted to order them. Since his book was about his western boyhood and was written as a tribute to his father and grandfather, making sure that it stayed in print was important to Bill. He used the word "legacy" several times as he told his story. He hadn't found an agent to broker the deal, but felt confident he had done the right thing by going it alone. "Agent or no agent, there's just not that much money to be had in the world of university presses," he said.

His publisher's willingness to keep the book around was certainly a plus, but Bill's deal also had downsides. His advance had been $5,000. Respectable for a small publisher, but not enough to make writing any more than a financial sideline for an author and certainly not enough to tempt an agent to get involved. Very little was planned in the way of publicity. Bill would be sent out to tour branches of the state university — this is Montana, remember — and he might be reviewed in area papers or alumni magazines, but that was about it. When Helena and I questioned him about plans for online marketing, such as blog tours, he looked at us blankly. In short, Bill's novel would be marketed as a regional book with modest expectations for sales.

Helena's experience was the dead opposite. She had a big-time agent who'd gotten her a $250,000 advance from a big-time editor at a big-time publishing house. A quarter of a million is an astounding amount for an untried author, and the publisher planned to recoup that investment through publicity. They were building Helena as a brand already, promoting her blog and introducing her as the "girl du jour" at a series of New York readings and events. Her book had been heavily edited — she said they'd lopped off the first fifty pages and excised a key character — and she had not been consulted about the title, cover, or how the book was being promoted. "I don't think they liked my book," she said, ducking her head, "as much as they liked the idea of my book."

On the plus side, she was getting a lot of money and a lot of attention. On the minus side, both she and her book were being turned into a commodity, and Helena was under tremendous pressure. She confessed she had thrown up every single day since she signed the contract and that she had recurring dreams about being in a car with no brakes. She knew this was her big shot. If this book didn't make it, the odds someone would gamble that kind of money and attention on a subsequent effort were almost nil.

My situation was somewhere in the middle. For my first novel, *Love in Mid Air*, I'd gotten a $65,000 advance from a medium-tier editor at a medium-sized house. My publisher had done a fantastic job of selling foreign rights, so that I was very nearly in the black before the book even rolled off the presses. There were some publicity plans, but not the full-court press expected for Helena's book. I'd been lightly edited and consulted about the title and cover, but it had been clear the final decision rested with the publisher.

So… who got the best deal?

As the fire died down, the wine sank in its bottle, and the shadows outside the window grew longer, the three of us continued to analyze and confess. The talk gradually turned from our deals to our fantasies and how well the realities of our situations were matching up to what we'd hoped for. It was clear that from the very start, we'd all wanted different things. While Bill had talked about his book being a "legacy," something for a seventy-eight-year-old man to leave behind him, Helena repeatedly used the word "launch." She was at the beginning of her career. She'd seen her equally ambitious friends precede her into publication, and she was eager to join them in what seemed to her to be a charmed circle of powerful people residing in the epicenter of the publication universe.

My dream involved the word "global." Where Bill wanted his work to go long and Helena wanted hers to vault high, the dimension I was seeking was breadth. Not only had I made a living as a travel writer, but my parents had been in the import business. Growing up I had traveled with them and, as a teenager, I used to go into bookstores in foreign cities and just wander around, looking at the incomprehensible covers and wondering who these people were. I had come back from one of these European trips and grandly announced to my high school friends that I now considered myself to be "a citizen of the world." So the foreign rights capacity of my publisher really mattered to me on a deep emotional level. The fact that people in Christchurch or Istanbul or Rotterdam would be reading my book was nothing short of intoxicating.

Have your feelings about who had the best deal changed at all?

Here's the point of the story. Selling and marketing a novel involves an extended series of choices and negotiations — more than any writer is ever prepared for. Sometimes you're making decisions without even consciously being aware that you are — and not being aware that a certain path is open to you is the same thing as opting not to take that path, at least in terms of results. When writers confront the publishing machine, they often roll into a fetal position, pretending these decisions aren't there to be made.

Most writers are so desperate to find an agent and sell their book that they don't realize that they need to be thinking analytically and strategically about their publication experience from the moment their books near completion. Don't get me wrong. I'm not suggesting that the writer is in total control of his or her process. We aren't. But while we don't have total control, we do have some control, and the decisions that we make early on are monumental in determining what will ultimately happen to our books and our careers. That's why the myths of publication are so dangerous. They imply that things simply either happen to writers... or they don't.

Denial is tempting — but dangerous. To say, "Because I don't have total control, I'm going to proceed as if I don't have any control," is the sort of thinking that short circuits writers before their careers even begin.

By now, probably quite a few questions have risen in your mind, such as, "How do you get into one of these swell artist colonies?" "What's a blog tour?" "How do foreign rights relate to an advance?" "What do you mean by 'midlist' and 'remaindered'?" and "Why the heck didn't somebody slap you when you referred to yourself as 'a citizen of the world'?" We'll discuss all this in the chapters to follow, but the key reason I started with this story is that my autumn afternoon with Bill and Helena illustrates three points:

1. Decisions are being made all the time, either by you or for you.

Upping your awareness early in the process will help you make smarter choices.

2. No publishing experience is perfect.

Writers want to believe there's some mythical deal out there that will give them everything they want... but trust me, it doesn't exist. Every decision has a flip side. If you get a big advance, you'll have pressure. If you get the multi-book deal, you'll have multi-deadlines. If you get the big tour, you'll spend lonely nights in hotels all over the country. If everybody's flattering you and calling you literary, all that means is that they aren't going to give you any money. Rather than chasing some unattainably perfect deal, think of it as a real estate transaction, i.e., a constant balancing between the dream in your head and the reality of what the market offers. If you show up at a realtor's office and say, "I want a house that's on ten acres but it needs to be an easy commute to my job uptown and, oh yeah, I want to pay fifty thousand dollars for it," they're not going to think you're a tough negotiator, they're going to think you're an idiot. Publishing is similar to buying a house — you'll need to analyze your priorities and make some tough calls about where you can compromise and where you can't.

3. In light of facts one and two, your time is best spent in negotiating for the things that matter most to you.

Of course, this requires you to know what matters to you... which is not as easy as it sounds, but my conversation with Bill and Helena helped me start to zero-in on my personal definition of success. Being the "girl du jour" in Brooklyn or doing a tour of the university system of Montana wouldn't have meant much to me, just as a Hebrew translation of their books may not have been an emotional hot button for Bill or Helena. Sometimes the best way to figure out what matters is to winnow out what doesn't matter. The things you can't bear to let go of become your list of non-negotiables.

I've stayed in touch with both Helena and Bill during the last three years. (We finally convinced Bill to try Facebook.) While there have been plenty of ups and downs, I think we all had a pretty good ride in the sense that while none of us got everything we wanted, we all got some of the things we wanted. And we all survived to write second novels, which in this nutty world is no small feat. The people who best navigate the publication process don't become swept up in the myths and fantasies, tempting as they might be. The people who function best are those who get bottom-of-the-bottle-of-wine honest with themselves about why they're doing this, what they really want out of it, and what they're willing to give up to attain that goal.

There are a lot of books on writing out there and many of them are excellent; that part of the journey is so well-documented that there's no need to cover it again. This guide will focus on what happens after your book is finished — navigating agents, editors, revisions, becoming your own publicist, surviving the rigors of a book tour or the sting of a bad review. It contains tips to help you balance the emotional highs and lows that come as you move from the solitary interior world of the writer into the chaotic public world of the author.

Publishing is changing so fast right now that we're bringing this book out using print-on-demand technology specifically so we can update frequently and can thus keep up with trends in self-publishing, ebooks, and ways authors are using the internet to find and interact with readers. Writers have options today that simply didn't exist a decade ago. We'll go through them chapter by chapter, helping you make the best decisions for you and your book.

Chapter One

So You Finished Your Book — Now What?

It gives me no sadistic pleasure to tell you this, but the odds are you really haven't finished your book. You just think you have.

There's a big difference between having a book that's finished in the sense you've reached a certain word count or come to the end of a draft and having a book that's ready to show in the marketplace. Before you send a manuscript out, you need to do everything in your power to make sure it's been polished and perfected. Writers sometimes erroneously believe that agents and editors exist to explain to them what's wrong with their books, or perhaps even to help them correct those faults. It would be nice if it worked that way, but in the real world, industry professionals are far too busy to be doctoring the manuscripts of strangers.

Agents and editors will generally only offer assistance to writers they've already taken under contract. If you've created three successful books in a row and are having a little problem with the opening chapter of book number four, then you can likely expect counsel from your agent. And if an editor has paid a tidy sum for your manuscript or an even tidier sum for a multi-book deal, then she indeed has a powerful incentive to make sure the books she's just bought are good. But if you're a novice writer, it's extremely unrealistic to expect an agent or editor to carefully read your manuscript, looking for hidden potential, and then spend years helping you craft a saleable book.

Consider the typical agent in New York. He has queries and sample chapters and full manuscripts all over his office, with more pouring in every day. (I once heard of an agent who worked out of her apartment and who was so overrun with manuscripts that she even had them stacked in the oven — but perhaps that's urban legend.) The typical agent doesn't read most of these queries, but rather farms them out to junior agents or interns for screening. Only the most promising work is passed along to the agent himself.

With so many writers to choose from, an agent will likely only take on a project that's well-written, compelling, complete, and one that he thinks he can sell. The first time his interest wanes or he encounters a rookie mistake, he will toss your manuscript aside and say, "Next."

There are exceptions to this rule, of course. If you are a scandal-ridden star of a reality TV show who just got impregnated by the NFL quarterback you met in rehab, the publishing industry will drop everything to get your memoir out by the time the baby is born. They'll help you so much, in fact, that you won't be required to do any actual writing. And occasionally you hear stories of a concept so incredibly gripping that an agent or editor took on a downright lousy manuscript and helped the writer turn it into a workable book. But this is rare. Really rare. You simply can't count on it. You may think your tale of a girl growing up in Kansas is heart-wrenching and unique, but if you're dealing with a mainstream theme, something else has to grab them: a snappy opening, a mesmerizing point of view, stellar writing — or all three.

You don't get many chances to impress an agent or editor, so you need to make each of those chances count. Manuscripts are accepted or rejected for all kinds of reasons, many of which you have no control over. You can't do anything about the general economy, or the fact fewer people are reading, or that this particular agent is overstocked with Midwestern coming-of-age stories and thus wouldn't take on your Kansas girl no matter how fetchingly she told her tale. But you can control the quality of your manuscript.

So, before you even think about sending anything to an agent, make sure your book is as strong as you can make it. These five steps will help you evaluate how far you have to go.

1. Read your book… out loud

You're probably thinking, "That will take forever."

It will, and that's the point.

If you believe you have a book that's anywhere near ready to go to market, you've undoubtedly taken it through multiple drafts and somewhere along the way you've probably numbed out to the prose. It can be very hard to read our own words analytically... we know all too well what's coming next, so we start to skim. We're flipping the pages so fast that we don't catch small issues like typos or larger ones like plot improbabilities.

Reading out loud slows you down. It allows you to approach each page as if someone else had written it. Tics in the writing begin to leap out at you — awkward phrasing, run-on or choppy sentences, a tendency to repeat the same word over and over.

When I first read the draft of my novel aloud, I was appalled by how often I used the word "surprise." I did a word search and found that not only did some variation of the word "surprise" appear 16 times in the manuscript, but that I seemed to have a special penchant for the term "somewhat surprisingly." Second place went to "suddenly," which was in there 11 times. Well, that explained it. No wonder people in my book were always surprised. Things were happening very suddenly!

Fortunately, the process of reading my book aloud alerted me to my embarrassing over-reliance on these words before I sent the manuscript out. A friend who also reads her chapters aloud realized she has a tendency toward long sentences. When she started reading her dialogue out loud, she found she couldn't get through certain lines without gasping for air. Lesson learned. If it's difficult to say, it's probably annoying to read.

(In a similar vein, some writers swear that they can look at their work through fresh eyes simply by printing it in a bizarre font. So if you're used to something serviceable and plain like Times New Roman, run a chapter out in Batik or Matisse and see if it reads differently to you.)

Reading your work aloud also makes you sensitive to the question of voice. Voice is the X-factor in literature and a lot of times when readers say, "I just didn't connect with this story," what they're really saying is that they weren't captivated by the voice. Voice is subjective, and therefore tricky. Not everyone responds to the same sort of narrative voice, so your smart-ass teenage anti-hero might score with some readers and irritate others. The important thing is that these words you're reading aloud actually sound like someone's voice, i.e., they have the rhythms and nuances of human speech. Reading out loud can tip you off to places where you've gotten too scholarly or detached, where you've slipped out of character, or lost conversational phrasing. It can be disconcerting to keep stopping in your reading and thinking, "Wow, that sounds awkward," but this is the time to catch it and fix it. If you find yourself reading with expression on the other hand, practically acting the scenes out as you turn the pages, then congratulations. That's a sign your voice is working.

2. Solicit feedback from amateur readers.

By "amateur" I mean people who aren't agents, editors, or teachers in an MFA program. It's up to you who you ask, but it's worth taking time to consider who might serve best in this crucial role of first readers.

I only show work-in-progress to other writers. A lot of my friends are writers, so it's an easy call to also make them my first readers. For other people, a group of avid booklovers works just as well. And some brave souls use their spouses, lovers, mothers, or siblings as first readers. It's really a matter of personal preference. I like using writers because once they tell you what they think isn't working — the beginning is slow, your narrator is coming off like a shrew, you have too many scenes of people sitting in restaurants talking — they often have suggestions for how you might correct this problem as well. I appreciate this sort of feedback, but some writers find it oppressive. They prefer getting raw reactions from people who represent their future readers, i.e., people who love books but aren't writers, and who thus aren't apt to offer so damn many suggestions.

But there's one group you definitely don't want as first readers: talented, even brilliant writers who can't quite seem to get working on anything of their own. They're blocked, they're torn between two projects, they're still recovering from the savage rejection they suffered in 1994, they're waiting until they get their office feng shui-ed or their eldest son gets out of juvie. The list of reasons that writers don't write is endless, but you can't afford to deal with any of these people right now. Yeah, I know they're smart and I know they have all kinds of time on their hands. They may even volunteer to read it. If they do, just mumble something vague about not being ready to show your work yet.

Blocked writers tend to be bad readers. They may unconsciously be jealous that you're actually doing what they're just talking about and thus be overly critical of your work. They, again unconsciously, may try to talk you into writing the book they can't write and then they'll come back with extraordinarily unhelpful advice, such as, "This story would work much better if it was set in Paris on the brink of World War I." Or they may be blocked because they're perfectionists and carry that same perfectionism to their read of your work, giving you a line edit when what you really need is a big-picture feedback.

How many first readers do you need? I'd say the perfect amount is between three and six. For starters, different people are going to catch different things, so you want some variety in your first reader circle. If you only have one or two people, any comments they make will have too much impact on your thinking. Let's say you have a rather graphic sex scene. If you only had one first reader and she objected to the scene, there's a chance that she's coming out of a personal place. Maybe she simply doesn't like direct sexuality in books, or maybe something about the scene was triggering for her, so cutting that scene based on a single person's read could well be a mistake.

But if four people read it and they all thought the scene was too much, you need to consider cutting it. Note that I said "consider." You don't have to cut it. First readers are just that, readers, not ultimate judges of your work. But if you show a manuscript to a variety of people and they all stumble over the same chapter or dislike the same character, you owe it to yourself to take their comments seriously. Nothing is worse than a writer who solicits feedback and then ignores it. Most often these people were pretending to want critiques when they really just wanted praise, and serious readers soon tire of working with divas, no matter how talented they might be.

At the other end of the spectrum, you don't want too many readers. If you show work to ten people you're likely to end up with such a mishmash of opinions that you'll be confused. Ellie loved the ending. Josh felt it faded out. Caroline felt the dialogue just needed some tweaking, and Mark insists that the real ending of the story is twenty pages earlier and the last chapter is superfluous. Too much feedback can be paralyzing, worse than none at all. If you try to incorporate everyone's suggestions, your book will end up with that "edited by committee" feel sometimes seen in books that were spawned in MFA programs and have been subsequently workshopped to death. These books don't have any mistakes but they also don't have any life. The author listened to everyone, taking out any possibly offensive, and therefore any unique, parts of the manuscript, and the result was a story with all the energy and individuality of a dial tone.

3. After you get all this feedback, sit on it for at least a month. Three is better.

I'm not kidding. A book is like a cake. You have to let it cool off thoroughly before you start to ice it, or the whole thing will come apart in your hands.

While you're waiting, it's fine to work on other projects. Maybe something short and fun as a reward for having completed the marathon task of writing a novel. And you may as well send these out for publication in magazines, journals, newspapers; don't wait until your book is published to find your readers. It's also a good time to read those other books that you've accumulated beside your bed — not just Austen and Dickens, but contemporary books that will give you some sense of how other writers have dealt with the challenges you face.

4. Reread the book, all in one day if possible.

Evaluate the feedback you've gotten from your first readers and incorporate only those suggestions that feel right to you.

5. Repeat steps 1-4.

Go through the cycle as many times as it takes until you know the book is absolutely as good as it can be.

Chapter Two

Networking

It's funny. Writing is a solitary task, but in order to succeed at it, you need other people. Not only does networking help you get a publicity system in place for when it's time to market your work, but, in the meantime, surrounding yourself with those who also love books keeps you motivated. So even though you conceived your dream of being a writer in private, it will take a virtual village to make that dream real.

But you need to make sure you're aligned with the right sort of people.

One of my favorite stories about writing isn't really about writing— it's about track and field. For years, trainers thought it was literally impossible for an athlete to run a mile in less than four minutes. Who knows exactly why they thought it was impossible — perhaps they envisioned muscles shredding under the pressure or hearts and lungs exploding from the stress. Then, in 1954, a British runner named Roger Bannister actually broke the four-minute mile—and, precisely 46 days later, someone else did too. Within a year, three more athletes had joined their ranks, and by the end of 1957, less than three years after Bannister had done the seemingly impossible, sixteen other runners had broken the four-minute mile.

What happened? Did a whole class of runners magically get faster?

A more likely scenario is that Bannister's feat had revealed the four-minute mile as a false barrier. Elite athletes are a tightly knit crowd. The odds are most of these runners knew Bannister, had raced against him before, and perhaps had even beaten him. They probably thought, "Hell, Bannister did it? He's not any faster than me!" The fact that the barrier had not only been broken, but broken by someone they knew, made it easier to visualize the four-minute mile as an actual goal. And once they got it out of their heads that it was impossible, sixteen of them did it.

Writing is like that too. False barriers abound and the people who believe in them can drag you down. Every MFA program, conference, or workshop seems to have a few cynical souls who sit around drinking coffee and crushing other people's dreams. They mutter things like, "It's all about who you know," "Publishing's dead anyway," or "Have you seen the best seller list? Only the hacks survive." It's the literary equivalent of saying that the four-minute mile is unbreakable, and people can linger for years in this kind of self-fulfilling prophecy.

You need to be around people who know that, while it's hard, publishing a book is possible. People who are working steadily toward doing just that. People who will precede you into publication, and, while this may sting at the time — "Hell, Andrea sold her novel? She's not any better than me…" — it will motivate you to sit down at your desk and get to it. Deciding who goes into your network should hinge on three simple questions: Does this person make me want to write more and better? Does he treat writing like a worthwhile way to spend my time, a quest that may end in publication? And, does he know enough about writing and publishing to make his feedback helpful?

Your writing support group should be composed of people who understand what you're going through — fellow writers, teachers, editors, and people connected to the publishing trade. This makes them inherently different from your family and friends who, although they undoubtedly love you and may even love your book, will just as undoubtedly say things to torture you, such as, "Have you hired an agent yet?" or "How much money do you think you'll make when the book is a best seller?"

The members of your support group may not live in your hometown, unless your hometown happens to be New York. A lot of these relationships are conducted by phone, email, Facebook, and the occasional glass of wine at a conference. An ideal network has at least three layers of intimacy, all of which serve different functions.

Circle One: Your Nearest and Dearest

My three primary readers — Alison, Dawn, and Laura — live in New York, Massachusetts, and Virginia, while I live in North Carolina. I met them all at writing conferences and the friendships grew from there. We talk frequently and have visited each other's homes. Dawn has found me a rent-free beach house for a writing retreat and listened to me panic even when I didn't even know exactly what I was panicked about. Laura has traveled with me through Italy and helped me navigate the waters of online publishing. Alison and I go back the farthest: she not only introduced me to her agent but is my daughter's godmother. I need these people for assistance that goes beyond the practical. They are the ones to whom I express my deepest doubts and fears.

Circle Two: Your Critique Group

I also have a secondary ring of support, which is my in-town critique group. We meet every two weeks in the coffee shop of a local bookstore to give each other feedback on chapters. We also have made introductions to agents, filmed each other's book trailers, invited each other to contribute to anthologies, and set up folding chairs at readings. Success for one member of the group means success for us all. As my grandfather used to say, a rising tide lifts all boats.

While I like everyone in this group and count a couple of the members as close friends, it's important to note that I look to this second ring of support for different things than I need from my inner circle of friends. There are seven people in the group, which seems a good size. Most of us are working on novels so we exchange chapters via email attachments before each meeting. Through the years the critiques have varied. We've had our comma Nazi — every group needs one — and a couple of other close readers who primarily give line edits. Others are more "big picture" readers, focusing on the story movement as a whole. That's a good thing. You don't want everyone bringing the same dish to the Sunday picnic. And most important of all, while our group is very honest about what's working and what isn't, we never sink into nastiness or derision.

Our meeting formula is as follows: Several days before the meeting we all send out our work online and the others read it, writing down any kind of commentary they see fit. We arrive at the bookstore at 7 and hold chit-chat to a minimum, usually getting underway by 7:10. Our leader chooses someone to go first. The person to the left of the featured writer offers up his feedback and then the person to his left goes and so forth, until everyone has weighed in on the work. Many groups follow the classic "Say what works and then say what doesn't work" pattern and that's fine; our group leans more toward giving macro-comments, i.e., overall impressions about whether or not the chapters are working, followed by micro-comments, i.e., pointing out reactions to particular lines or word choices that we especially liked or especially didn't.

The person whose work is being critiqued does not speak unless asked a direct question. The author can say whatever he or she likes at the end, but not during the critique. Most serious groups hold to this rule, because you don't want the writer jumping in saying things like, "Oh, but I'm going to explain all that in the next chapter." To use a critique group correctly you have to remember that they aren't there to flatter or reassure you. They're there to represent the reader. If a line stops them cold, a character's reaction doesn't feel true, or they just don't buy where the story is going, you need to sit silently and hear them out. You may or may not agree with their opinions — after all, as we've said before, one reader is just one reader. But you do need to respect and value the information they're giving you, especially as it relates to things that are unclear. After all, when someone someday buys your book and takes it home, you won't be sitting there beside them as they read, saying, "Trust me, this all clears up on page 87."

After one person is critiqued, we move on to the next. With this many people in the group and a two-hour time limit, we maintain a pretty swift pace. Some groups only critique one or two writers per meeting to allow more time. It totally depends upon the dynamics of each particular group and how much material the writers in that group can produce in the time span between meetings.

Just as a good critique group doesn't necessarily hinge on friendship, nor does it require that everyone in it is working on similar material. Three of the people in my group are science fiction or fantasy writers, genres I know very little about. Throughout the years we've had a woman who focused on historical romance, another who wrote thrillers, and several people who write mainstream/literary fiction. The disparity in our subject matter is actually an advantage to the group because sometimes we give each other perspectives that are real eye-openers.

For example, the sci-fi/fantasy writers in the group often make points about plot or pacing that would never have occurred to me. Nor, I suspect, would it have occurred to Alison, Dawn, or Laura, who also reside in the more character-driven world of literary fiction. While your first circle is probably composed of writers with whom you have a lot of similarities, your second circle needs to bring in more variety. Not all of the comments I get from the sci-fi/fantasy guys are apt, just as I suspect not all of my artsy-fartsy observations are useful to them. But sometimes this out-of-genre feedback not only hits home but helps you to see your material in a totally different way.

Another thing you don't need to share is a zip code. Some of the most effective groups meet online. Writers who have met simpatico readers at conferences and workshops often opt to continue those relationships in virtual critique groups once they're all home. In fact, I would argue that the most lasting benefits of these experiences — even MFA programs — aren't garnered inside the classrooms but rather in the social hours that follow. Finding good readers is a huge boon to your career and will probably have a greater long-term payoff than the actual classes.

If you simply can't get to a conference, you can try finding a writing group in your own home town. It's probably a good idea to meet people personally before you exchange work. When you join a group because you've seen a flyer on a coffee shop wall or an ad in a pick-up magazine, you're taking a chance that the people you encounter will be damn weird, even by writer standards. My friend Mike showed up at a critique group in Atlanta only to find it was completely populated by people who wanted to rip apart current best sellers, not discuss their own — probably nonexistent — books.

What you do need to have in common with the other people in your critique group is that, a) everyone is writing, and b) everyone is writing at approximately the same pace, at least to the degree that they all submit pages nearly every meeting. Life is unpredictable and everyone skips occasionally, but be wary of members who happily critique the work of others while never submitting anything of their own. A writing group should be a level playing field with everyone swapping roles, and if you aren't willing to be judged by your peers, you've forfeited the right to judge them.

What you most want to avoid is a writing group where no one does any actual writing.

This happened to me early in my fiction career. I found myself in a group of women who had all come together through a creativity camp based on Julia Cameron's book *The Artist's Way.* We enjoyed each other's company so much that it was months before I realized I was the only one who regularly brought in pages. Our meetings were fun. Their houses were lovely. They served home-made scones. We had kick-ass Christmas parties where we exchanged clever, carefully selected gifts. We took road trips to the beach. I didn't want to leave this group, so at first I tried to cajole my friends into writing more. We tried meeting more frequently, then less frequently. Over time it became clear that not only was I the only one writing, but I was the only one who cared about the fact I was the only one writing.

So, you're probably thinking, why didn't I just relax and accept the meetings for what they were — a social outing?

But here's the problem with being in a writing group that doesn't write. After a while you stop writing too. It begins to seem like an increasingly foolish activity and you begin to feel like the nerd who stayed home and worked on a term paper while all her friends were at the movies. I could have accepted the group as social if we'd started out that way, but since we'd sworn to hold each other to a certain pace and standard of work, the fact we failed to do this made the whole experience go a little sour. I had to leave the group, but I'm happy to report that I retained several of the women as friends.

It was years before I felt like joining another group, and the reason that my present group works for me — despite its tragic lack of scones and beach trips — is that these people are all writing on a regular basis. Steady and democratic production is the single most important factor in making a critique group work.

Circle Three: Your Publicity Web

I realize that the whole idea of a publicity web may sound a little calculating, but please, don't stop reading. This is a huge part of what it takes to be a successful author in the modern era.

Deep breath. Still with me? Good.

Your publicity web is composed of the people who will help you get out the word once your book is published. It's composed of:

People who read your blog and people whose blogs you read.

People from your MFA program, if you attended one.

Facebook friends and Twitter followers.
People you met at colonies, conferences, or workshops.
Members of your writing group.

There are many reasons why you shouldn't isolate yourself as a writer, but one of the biggest is that writers also read and they know people who read, and you'll need access to these readers down the road. Don't think you can wait until you have a book contract in your hot little hand to start building your web. Things move very fast once the contract is signed, and this is one task you can begin doing now, while you have more time. Also, writers who work the internet are legitimately suspicious of people who never participate until they have a book coming out and who suddenly become a mega-presence, posting, tweeting, and messaging constantly. Needless to say, once their books are launched, these fair-weather internet friends disappear as fast as they originally appeared, and other writers brand them as precisely what they are — users.

So… get your blog going now. There's no reason not to, when it's so simple and cheap to build a blog presence. Details on how to do this are in Chapter 10.

Some bloggers post every day but that can become burdensome if you're also trying to write a book, and besides, you don't want to bludgeon readers with too much too fast. At the other end of the spectrum, if you only post once a month, readers will forget about you. Once or twice a week is a nice compromise. Some blogs have a set theme, others are more loose and almost diary style. The smartest thing is to peruse lots of writing blogs and see what attracts you. Start following the ones you like.

Then begin friending other writers on Facebook.

I caught on to the magic of this in a rather bizarre way. My book was scheduled to debut in March, and on January 3 of that year, the first working day of 2010, I woke up, stumbled to my computer, and turned it on. There, in my inbox, was a letter from my editor with the subject line STARRED REVIEW IN PUBLISHER'S WEEKLY.

Publisher's Weekly is an important force and, since they're the first review to come out on upcoming books, they carry a disproportionate degree of power, almost as if they're a harbinger of things to come. They only give a star to a small percentage of the books they review, so this was a big deal, a very good sign, the ideal way to start the new year.

It went to my head. It was like 6:30 in the morning, still dark outside and way too early to call family and friends. So I got on Facebook and started sending friend requests to famous writers, people I admired but would have never previously had the courage to approach. Nicole Krauss, Tom Perrotta, Amy Bloom, Lorrie Moore, Benjamin Percy… I was in a friending frenzy.

Most of them friended me back. And then I started friending their friends. Facebook can be very helpful in these situations, because each time I friended someone, I was automatically introduced to some of their friends, many of whom were also writers. Within a month I had over 300 writers as friends and each time I went to Facebook I had the option of entering a discussion about writing and publishing. I went from silence to endless chances for conversation, and since I really looked at people's pages before I sent out a friend request, the process wasn't quite as willy-nilly as it sounds. I ended up with a list of people I had a lot in common with, writers whose work I admired, whose concerns I identified with, and whose sense of humor I enjoyed.

After launching a blog and building your presence on Facebook, the next step is to connect these two threads. Invite your Facebook friends to follow your blog. Each time you write a new blogpost, announce your topic on Facebook. Before you get very far in this process, you'll find that online friendships are like any other, and you'll hit it off with some people more than others. Many bloggers have lists of other blogs they like and follow on their pages; if you like their blog, the odds are you'll like the ones they recommend, so click on them and check them out. And then begin to recommend blogs you like on your blog. Likewise, if you friend someone and find yourself enjoying their posts, the odds are that you'll enjoy their friends. Anyone who has more than 50 friends in common with you is a likely bet. See how rapidly this web can expand?

It's important to note that simply announcing on Facebook that you've published a book doesn't automatically bump your sales. An April 2011 survey by *Poets & Writers* showed that only 2% of respondents said they'd found the last book they read via Facebook or Twitter. Facebook and Twitter are best used to introduce people to your blog and others who feature your work. Twitter, which holds you to a puny 140 characters per message but allows you to build a following insanely fast, is best used to direct people to other things, such as a link to a website or blogpost you admire. Once your book is published and you have news of your own to announce, it's the best way to toot your own horn. And blog posts — perhaps because they offer a peek inside the mind of the writer, something many readers enjoy — are an excellent way to establish a readership. Almost inevitably, the days I am featured in a blog, I notice a rise in my online sales.

Remember to comment on other people's blogs and Facebook posts and to re-tweet their tweets on Twitter. You can't just be the gaping mouth of need, constantly expecting people to respond to what you've written, but never taking the time to comment on their posts. If you someday hope these people will review your book or interview you on their blog, then the only decent thing to do is to first review their books or offer to interview them on yours. It's not just a matter of being willing to reciprocate for any attention they give your work, although even this is better than some bloggers who demand attention but never share the limelight. The truly classy thing to do is to go first, using your new blog platform to showcase the work of fellow writers or helping them to get lively discussions going by commenting on their posts. When your book hits the scene, the odds are they'll be happy to help you.

Since *Love in Mid Air* has come out, one of the great surprises has been how much other authors have been willing to help me publicize my book. Like most writers, I'd been burned through the years by my share of bitchy critiques and hyper-competitive conferences, so I was surprised to enter this Eden of writers who encourage and comfort their fellow artists. There's always a bit of elbow-slinging and nastiness at the bottom of the ladder and perhaps people become mean again at the top, I don't know. But in the middle of the publishing ladder I have found extraordinary kindness.

Ready for a shower?

So is friending, blogging, critiquing, reviewing, and commenting on literary threads just one big cynical game?

No, not really.

It just feels weird at first.

Building a writing network is a fluid process. My nearest and dearest all started as casual acquaintances I met at conferences. People you meet at a book signing or people who responded to the same post online can end up becoming members of your critique group and, in turn, true confidants. It isn't that your entire social network needs to be composed of writers; most of us, I suspect, desperately need a life outside of this business. One of the things I've come to appreciate about my family is that they don't really understand how publishing works. There are days when I'm happy to leave it at "How's the book going?" and "Just great!" So saying that you build a network of writing contacts is not saying that you'll turn your back on your old friends. But it's really wonderful to develop writing buddies and to see these new relationships deepen over time.

And actually doing all this is easier and more organic than it sounds. When you meet someone you like at a conference, it will begin to feel natural to go home and friend them or invite them to guest post in your blog, then peruse their own lists of writing friends. Friends of friends of friends is how this business works. It's only phony if you're faking interest in people's opinions and problems or if you expect them to do favors for you but you're unwilling to help them in return — and my guess would be neither of these things are true. The vast majority of writers thrive on this sort of give and take.

It's just that now you're making friends in a more conscious manner. Like the new kid in school — and, if you want to publish, you are precisely that, the eternal new kid in an eternal new school — you have to work harder to become part of the group.

My beloved friend Alison hates all this. Of course, Alison lives in Brooklyn, where you can't shoot a rubber band without hitting a writer, so it's easier for her. If you're in Omaha or Tacoma or Duluth — or Charlotte, like I am — it takes a little more effort and thus can make you feel a little more self-conscious. But even if the process is contrived, the relationships that arise from it are real. Alison always says, "What if we don't call all this networking? What if we just call it friendship?"

She makes an excellent point.

Chapter Three

Conferences, Workshops, and MFA Programs

Okay, now it's time to be a little bolder. In order to make it, books have to go out into the big wide world and so do their authors. Let the journey begin!

Conferences

Conferences can have an enormous impact on your career, but the type you choose depends on where you are in that career, and how much you're willing to test yourself.

Lecture-Style Conferences

Most people start small, in their hometown. They maybe join a local writing or library group that brings in speakers and sponsors roundtable discussions. College alumni groups are often good bets as well, as are readings at area bookstores. This is easy, since all you have to do is sit there and listen, and the speakers are often quite helpful. Most of these events are free and if there are fees, they are generally modest.

Some "sit there and listen" conferences are much larger, such as the annual meeting of the Association of Writers and Writing Programs (www.awp.org), which hosts a giant four-day event in a different city each year. Many big-name writers attend the AWP, so be prepared to gawk at your favorite literary crush, and there are a staggering amount of discussions and readings to choose from. Many colleges, cities, and states hold annual book festivals as well, another good chance to hear authors read from their work or listen to a panel of first-time writers discussing how they got started.

Some of these larger events offer lectures where the speakers go into more detail about matters of craft, but the students aren't required to show their own work. This format appeals to people who are seeking basic information but who aren't ready for critique. In other words, beginners.

Workshop-Style Conferences

If you're serious about this publishing thing, eventually you'll need to try a workshop-style conference. Most of these conferences run ads in *Poets & Writers* magazine, or you can do an online search under "writing conferences." The following sites offer lists of conferences organized by location or date, along with links to each conference website:

www.pw.org
writing.shawguides.com
www.newpages.com/writing-conferences

The workshop-style conference represents a more significant commitment than the lecture-style, since they generally last one or two weeks, cost from a few hundred to a few thousand dollars, and require you to travel to the college campuses where they're held, which are almost inevitably twenty-eight miles from nowhere. In addition, the big name conferences — Bread Loaf, Sewanee, and Tin House, to name a few — require you to apply. Not everyone gets in and, even if you do, there's no guarantee you'll study with the instructor of your choice.

For example, let's look at the MacDaddy of them all, Bread Loaf, a ten-day conference held every summer in Vermont. Despite a cost of $2620 for tuition, lodging, and food, the prestige of Bread Loaf is so undeniable that they get a lot of applicants. Their 2011 webpage reported that a mere 23% of applicants got in and only 6% of them received financial aid.

Not all of them are quite so scary, and each conference has its own special gestalt. Iowa has a famous faculty, but isn't hard to get into, a situation that caused one former attendee to sniff, "the students are neither especially talented nor especially serious. College towns are full of bars and half my class spent the week drunk." Florida's Eckerd College hosts Writers in Paradise, and since mystery superstar Dennis Lehane is co-director, they're known for having a more commercial focus, bringing in best-selling writers to speak. Stephen King was even there one year. Some conferences are in such great locales they qualify as mini-vacations: Maui, Napa Valley, Provincetown, Taos, and Key West leap to mind. And some are specifically known for their reassuring vibe. At Table Rock and Wildacres, two small conferences in the North Carolina mountains, students eat their meals with the faculty, who've been chosen not just on the basis of their teaching ability but also their warmth and accessibility.

There's a conference to suit every level and every need, so go to the sites listed above and then click on the webpages of individual conferences. They'll give you the basics — schedule, faculty, location, cost, and admission requirements — but the real trick is to read between the lines and get a sense of personality. Soon enough you'll be able to tell if it's a party campus, a feel-good singalong, or a cutthroat-serious marketplace — or if the focus is on inspiring beginners, developing works in progress, or selling completed manuscripts.

My friend Angie, an MFA grad and veteran of many conferences, says she evaluates on this criteria:

1. Length and schedule

How much time do you actually spend in the workshops? In student critique groups? Having one-on-one evaluations with your teacher? At readings? Some students like a jam-packed schedule while others want time to write built into their conference day.

2. TEACHER ACCESSIBILITY

"Some conferences advertise big name authors," Angie says, "but they only come in for a few hours to do a reading and signing then disappear. It's crucial to check out how much actual time you'll be spending with the faculty."

3. DO THEY BRING IN AGENTS AND EDITORS?

Some do, some don't. Whether or not you'd benefit from spending the last day of your conference looking for representation depends on where you are in your career. If you don't have a finished manuscript, pitching to professionals is pointless.

4. HOW TOUGH IS IT TO GET IN?

If this is your first conference, a tight admission ratio like the one at Bread Loaf could lead to disappointment. But if you're more experienced, you might see it as a good screening system, guaranteeing the other students are as serious as you.

5. LOCATION

Not only do you want to be in a nice place, but location affects both the cost and length of your commute. A writer starting out in Gila, New Mexico will have to take every form of transportation short of a rickshaw to get to Bennington, Vermont and will burn days in the journey. Many attendees report that their transportation costs add as much as a thousand dollars to the overall price of their conference.

6. COST

Enough said. Only you know how much you're prepared to invest in this process. Some programs do offer scholarships and financial aid, but most students swallow the whole cost.

Whatever you decide, you need to get moving on this earlier than you'd logically think, because the turnaround time on conference acceptance is slow. You might decide you're a great fit for Sewanee, which, like most conferences, meets in the summer when the college kids are gone. But you'll still need to start your application process in the winter. The top-drawer conferences require writing samples, first to get accepted and then in order to match you with the right teachers and instruction levels. So give yourself plenty of time to craft and polish those twenty perfect pages.

I hope I haven't scared you away from the whole experience. The workshop type of conference will likely be your first step into the reality of writing, and for most people who attend them, they're transformative experiences. In some ways, the fact they aren't easy to get to or get into is part of the magic; applying requires real faith in yourself and is a sign you're ready to test-drive your writing dreams.

Story time. The first significant event in my long journey to become a novelist was to attend a two-week conference at Bennington College in Vermont. I'd written this bizarre, pop-culturish little short story called "Flipping" about a depressed woman who falls into her TV screen and begins interacting with characters from old sit-coms. I sent it in with my application, so naïve that I didn't even understand it was an application. I thought going to a conference was like checking into the Hilton. You sent in your money and told them when you were going to show up. Right?

Getting there was one obstacle after another. My kids were young, so being away for two weeks, especially in the summer when they were out of school, required calling in all my chips with my mom, mother-in-law, and friends. The fees were lower then, but spending twelve hundred dollars to nurture a career that existed only in my own mind seemed like the height of folly. Nonetheless, I farmed out the kids, wrote the check, packed up my jeep, and headed north.

I arrived at Bennington's campus, which was so New-England-college perfect it could have been a movie set, and was immediately hit upon by a fellow writer whom I mistook for a member of the welcome committee. He showed me to the nun-like austerity of my dorm room, and, once I figured out what was really going on, I showed him the door. I was left with the kind of thundering silence new mothers rarely find and a huge stack of papers that represented the work of my fellow classmates. I spent the afternoon reading their writing samples and — judging by the stillness in the hall — everyone else was doing the same. My anxiety faded a bit as I read. Fancy-shmancy Bennington or not, the quality of the writing was all over the place and my fervent prayer of "Just don't let me be the worst" was answered. Most of the time it's like this in almost any setting: you can find plenty of people who are ahead of you on the path and plenty who are behind. I've spent the subsequent fifteen years feeling pretty much as I did on that hot summer afternoon in Vermont — like I'm in the middle of the pack.

During my quick read-through, two of the manuscripts stood out. They weren't necessarily the best written or most polished, but I identified with their subject matter and felt that their authors, like me, were plowing the field of baby boomer suburban discontent. Now, from a thematic standpoint that's a pretty big field and I've since realized there are a lot of us in it, but at the time it seemed amazing to me to have found two other women who were also writing about crazy housewives. I took note of their names and, at the organizational meeting our class was having just before dinner, I made a point to pick them out of the group during introductions.

Later I was going through the line in the cafeteria, sort of marveling that I was back in a college cafeteria at all, and just as I was picking up my tray, I heard someone call out "Kim?" I turned to see the two women whose work I'd admired sitting together at a table and motioning for me to join them. Apparently they'd noticed the same similarities that I had, and that's just how simple — and how complex — the sorting process is. That moment standing there at the end of the cafeteria line was a real turning point in my life, and powerful enough that a modified version of it worked its way into my first novel, *Love in Mid Air.* It's a heady moment when you finally begin to find your tribe.

It's appropriate this all happened in a cafeteria, because critique-based conferences are a lot like high school. But this time you've landed in a very strange high school, where the smart kids are the cool kids, and cliques are formed not on the basis of the shoes you're wearing, but rather on how well you can write. Literary conferences may be the last meritocracy left on earth. You can't begin to tell who's talented just by looking at them, so the first classes are always full of surprises. There's always some self-impressed New Yorker with a name like Adrienne who's the last person in America who still smokes and who keeps running out at every break to talk on her phone, presumably to Kate Medina and Salman Rushdie and people way more important than you. But then the day comes when her work is up for critique and it turns out there's just one little crack in her armor — the girl can't write for shit. And then there's this terrified, chubby woman named Wanda who works someplace like the Fort Wayne, Arkansas DMV. She stands up to read dressed in a sweatshirt embroidered with the names of her grandkids and, lo and behold, she is among the blessed of the earth.

It's good for you to see this firsthand, that great writing might come from anyone and that talent really has nothing to do with where you were educated or who you know. Paranoia can attack a writer at almost any point in the process and, once you have your long-awaited contract in hand, it practically leaps out of the bushes at you. Good books go unnoticed while lesser ones sell like crazy, and it's easy to lose the innocence of the original dream, that writing well is its own reward. At times like this, it helps to look back to that image of Wanda, grandly holding court at her table in the cafeteria, while Adrienne slinks off friendless with her phone still pressed to her ear.

The feedback of your instructor matters too, of course. Some conferences place you in certain groups based on your application sample, but many leave it to the student to request. So when you're looking at a conference webpage or brochure and trying to decide which class is best for you, do a little research on the instructor.

Who you study with is more important than what you study. It's easy to Google the instructors and see what they've written and where they've taught and, since many writers have blogs, you can sometimes even get a glimpse at their personality. But be aware that even with research, choosing a teacher is a bit of a crapshoot. Teaching and writing are different skills; some famous writers aren't great teachers, while writers you've never heard of may be excellent in the classroom. Then there's the question of how hands-on their teaching style will be; some direct every aspect of their workshops while others take a more egalitarian approach, letting the students dictate much of what goes on.

No matter whom the person is, once you're at the conference, look for ways to get as much contact as you can with your instructor and the other faculty members. This may be a matter of simply asking questions in class or screwing up your courage to join them for a glass of wine before dinner. If your conference has a night where students read from work in progress, sign up to do this. I know of one woman who, after her reading, was approached by the instructor of another workshop who offered to introduce her to his agent. This is the uber-dream — that your work will be so outstanding you'll be plucked from obscurity and catapulted straight to the top — and on extremely rare occasions it does happen. Usually, interacting with faculty members and reading your work leads to more modest triumphs, like information, contacts, and the chance to practice reading aloud. It's still worthwhile. Everything that happens at the conference is one more chance to learn where your strengths are and what you need to keep working on.

It's intense, I know. There are always a few people who arrive, look around, and quietly leave. There are usually a few more who arrive, get their first critiques, and loudly leave. Even if you're prepared for the anxiety these conferences can stir up in writers, the odds are that by about day four you'll become so over-stimulated that you'll have to drive into town to the Olive Garden just for an hour of peace. That's fine. It's normal and even advisable to take little breaks, especially if you feel yourself getting jumpy or weepy. But remember that you didn't pay all this money and travel all this distance to hide. Get back into the flow of the conference as soon as possible. Ask questions and listen. Test yourself as much as you can bear.

Why? Because the feedback you get at a good conference can be career-changing. Back to Bennington. When I came in for my individual conference with my instructor Catherine Texier, who was very French and very intimidating, she pushed my little story about the crazy housewife across her desk and said "Well, you definitely have a voice…"

A voice? I had a voice? She may as well have anointed my head with oil. I don't remember anything else she said during our talk, but I remember this first sentence and it has sustained me more times than I can count. It has also, to some extent, defined me as a writer, because she was right. Voice is one of my strengths and I'm not sure I would have realized that so early without her help. This is not to say that all the feedback you receive at a conference is valid and helpful. Some conferences are better than others, some teachers are more gifted, some readers more astute, but at almost any conference, unless you've stumbled into a total stinker, someone will say something that resonates. It may be one of your strengths or it may be a weakness, but it will hit you with the force of truth and inform your work from that point on.

The minute I got home from Bennington I began researching conferences for the next year. I wound up at Wesleyan, in Connecticut, which is where I met my friend Alison, and for that reason alone it was more important to my career than Bennington would ultimately be. For several years afterwards, while my kids were growing up, I was limited to a conference a year so I tried to choose carefully and make the most of them. Some will yield more than others but that's part of the process. You have to be willing to just throw yourself out there.

And for ten solid years I kept my Bennington student ID in my purse, in the same little side flap where I put my driver's license, so that I would see it and touch it often. It was a talisman, something I was given the first day of my journey, and it helped me to remember, even when writing a check at the grocery, that I was a writer. If a conference does no more than teach you that, it can be worthwhile.

Pitch Conferences

The last type of conference is the most brutal. It's the pitch conference, sometimes called a pitch-and-shop or a pitch-and-sell. These conferences exist for people who have already finished a book, already workshopped and polished it, and who believe, rightly or wrongly, that it's time to take this little piggy to market. Pitch conferences are considerably cheaper than workshop conferences, averaging about $300, and they rarely occur on bucolic college campuses in small towns across the country. They're most often in New York or some other large city and they usually last only a day or two.

The reason is that the organizers bring in agents and editors to meet with the writers, so the conferences need to be close to where these agents and editors live, like New York. Time is of the essence at these conferences, which often echo the rat-a-tat pace of real-world publishing.

Although some feature speakers or offer a few classes to get everyone warmed up, pitch conferences are more about selling than writing, and the majority of attendees already have a finished book in hand. Usually there are two main parts to the process. First, instructors help you develop your actual pitch, which is two or three lines designed to get a stranger interested in your book. Sometimes it's called an "elevator pitch," because the idea is to pretend you are on an elevator with a power agent and you only have a few floors to sell yourself before he's gone forever.

Pitches not only have to be fast, but sharp. Many start with a question. When Laura was looking for a publisher for her YA (young adult) novel she came up with this tagline: "What if a sassy tooth fairy whisked a sensible girl off to the realm called Nearandfar only to discover the girl had more power than the fairies?" Laura likes the "What if..." model and points out that the editors and agents who will be ultimately hearing all these pitches will in turn have to sell these books to other people. If they are agents, they'll have to sell them to editors and if they are editors they'll have to convince their publisher that this book is a good bet. Either way, as Laura says, "When you come in with a pitch, you've done some of their work for them. You've given them not only a way to understand your book, but to in turn explain it to others."

Other pitches imitate the classic Hollywood model, implying your book is the fusion of two other well-known books, ala, "Dracula meets Huckleberry Finn." A variation of this is to compare your book to a current best-seller, then point out how it's different. "If The Girl with the Dragon Tattoo was set in Israel..."

Whatever you say, the goal of a pitch is to get the main idea across fast.

Once you've come up with your pitch, you often get the chance to test drive it on your fellow students. Some conferences also help you craft query letters, which you read aloud to the group and whenever someone loses interest they call out "Stop!" Needless to say, this little exercise isn't for the faint of heart, but the process is designed to emulate the way the query system actually works; presumably the agent tosses your letter aside the second his interest wanes, so you need to know where your weak spots are now.

After you've revamped your pitch and/or query, they bring in the actual professionals. Usually they are agents, but sometimes thrown into the mix are PR people or editors from small presses, the kind who buy directly from unagented authors. It's a bit like speed dating. You have a couple of minutes to interest the professional in your concept and then the whistle blows and they're on to the next person. Most conferences allow you to speak to two or three professionals and ideally they make some effort to match you with the most likely buyers. In other words, if, like Laura, you have a YA novel, there's no point in pitching to someone who represents exclusively non-fiction. Sometimes this system works better than others, so if the conference provides you with a list of attending agents in advance, do a little research and request the ones you consider your best shot.

The goal is to intrigue an agent or editor sufficiently well that he or she will ask to see the entire manuscript. But even if a professional likes your pitch, that's no guarantee that the road before you will be straight or smooth. One author I know met an editor at a pitch conference who showed interest in her work, but it wasn't until the writer worked for over a year with her agent — whom she'd met at a previous pitch conference — that the editor bought the book.

Even so, meeting an agent or editor face-to-face, even for a New York minute, is far better than simply sending your work through the slush pile. In subsequent contacts with that person you can say, "As you may recall, I met you at the Ratatat Conference last May and we discussed..."

One other thing about pitch conferences: maintain a healthy level of caution. When a college or university hosts a conference, their academic reputation is on the line and they try hard to provide their attendees with a worthwhile experience. You may not find the agent of your dreams, but at least you know you're not being played.

Pitch conferences, in contrast, sometimes load their rosters with what I call "faux agents" or "under editors." The conference organizers want people to leave happy, so the professionals who meet with the writers may have agreed to request to see a certain percentage of the projects presented to them. One conference advertised that one third of the attendees at their previous session met agents who requested to see their books. That's a suspiciously high percentage.

Since everyone at these things knows what's happening to everyone else — people who've been invited to submit work usually emerge from the meeting rooms jumping around and squealing like contestants who have just made the cut for *American Idol*—the fact that some people win makes the game seem legit. Those who didn't get chosen might figure they just need to work harder and come back to the next conference in a few months.

What the writers don't know is that the people sitting across the table may rank so low on the ladder back at their agencies or publishing houses that they couldn't take them on even if they wanted to. They work at agencies, yes, but they handle foreign rights or subsidies or work under the real agents; in short, they're simply not in a position to sell books. They work for publishers, yes, but in publicity, a field that doesn't have much to do with acquisitions. Or they may come from agencies/publishers that are so financially shaky or disconnected entirely from the publishing world that even if they take you on as a client, they don't have a prayer of selling your book.

Worst of all, these so-called professionals may be utter cynics who show up at conferences, agree to request a certain percentage of manuscripts, pocket their fee, and then, after a few weeks have passed, send them all back unread with "Sorry" scrawled across the bottom of the page.

It's sad but true. An entire subculture has mushroomed around the publishing business, designed to bilk writers.

If you're reading this, I assume you know enough about publishing that you would never pay an agent to read your work. Legitimate agents do not charge fees. But it can be harder to ascertain if an agent has been indirectly paid by the organizer of a conference, and that this is the only reason he's requesting your manuscript.

So how do you tell a faux agent from the real thing? The primary agenting association, the Association of Authors Representatives (www.aaronline.org) is a somewhat helpful screening device since it does at least require that its members have two years of experience in the field. But this doesn't mean they're selling books. The only real way to tell the fakes from the legits is to look at what, if anything, they have sold.

When it's time to market your book, go to www.publishersmarketplace.com and join. It's $20 a month, which is peanuts, because this site is a wealth of information. (Plus, it's a month-to-month commitment, so once your agent search is behind you, it's easy to cancel your membership.) First of all, a function called "Who Represents Who" tells you just that; if you admire a certain writer, you can quickly find out who her agent is. And if you're thinking of going with a certain agent, you can also peruse a list of his writers. Just as importantly, it's easy to research everything a certain agent has sold within a year. You can see who the author is, who the acquiring editor is, and get an approximate price range on how much the book sold for.

Not every agent reports every deal to *Publisher's Marketplace*, and because it's voluntary, some sales slip between the cracks. But if you search for an agent and see she hasn't sold anything in the last year or two, that's a bad sign. You want to find agents who are selling several projects a year, ideally to the kinds of editors and houses you admire. An agent may have sold twenty romances, but if you write mysteries, she's probably not the best choice for you.

Another option is to weed out the faux agent: if an agent requests a full manuscript, it's entirely legitimate to ask, "Who are some of the writers you represent? Would they be willing to talk with me?" A successful agent has good relationships with her writers and won't find this a strange request — in fact, he'll be happy to ask a client or two to call you. (They won't give out phone numbers and email addresses, of course, and you don't want them to. Once they're representing you, you'll expect the same level of caution, right?) But if an agent has either no clients or a stable of disgruntled clients, you'll figure this out fast.

Don't get me wrong. Most of the agents and editors who appear at conferences are legitimate. (And if you meet an agent at a conference sponsored by a university or MFA program, they're almost definitely legitimate. It's the one-day, big-city slugfests that get a little dicey.) Also, there's nothing inherently wrong signing on with an agent who isn't based in New York; some agents commute back and forth regularly and run thriving businesses from D.C. or L.A. or Chicago. Nor is there any reason why you should automatically avoid an agent who is simply young and untried. Everyone has to start somewhere, and a hungry new agent at a big house will likely pay your book far more attention than her hyper-busy comrades. But remember that most agents have thousands of writers vying for their attention, so the odds are small that an established agent will appear at one of these conferences in the first place. It's not a terrible thing to sign with a newbie agent, but you need to know what you're getting into from the start.

MFA Programs

Do you need an MFA ? That's a Master of Fine Arts degree, and if you simply want to publish and aren't concerned about making additional money by teaching, the short answer is "No." A lot of published writers don't have an MFA. I don't have one. Neither do my trusty comrades, Laura, Alison, and Dawn. And we've all managed to get our books into the hands of readers.

So you don't need one... but you might want one. MFAs give you a gift of uninterrupted time in which you can hone your craft, meet other writers, contemplate exactly what genre or material most speaks to you, and concentrate on long-term material like a novel. Just as many successful writers don't have an MFA, many successful writers do… and they often credit the MFA experience with building their confidence and expertise.

You can find MFAs listed in *Poets and Writers* magazine — I swear, they don't pay me for all these plugs — or search for them online. Like conferences, each MFA program has its own personality — some are so artsy and abstract they almost look down on the publishing industry while others are overtly oriented towards getting their graduates into print, frequently inviting agents and editors to visit the campus looking for marketable projects. Some, like Iowa and Columbia, are fiercely competitive both in terms of how many applicants they accept and in terms of what is expected of the students once they arrive. Others are known for a laid-back gestalt and allow students to snake through the program at their own pace, almost to the point where they become like a summer camp for adults — a safe place to hide for a few years while you consider the future of your marriage, read those Russian classics you somehow missed in college, and drink.

Personality aside, MFAs come in two main breeds. The first is the full residency MFA, which requires you to live on or near the college campus for the length of the program, which is usually one or two years. Needless to say, this is difficult for many returning students who have jobs and families, so low-residency MFAs are a popular alternative. Most require students to visit for a week each semester, and this adds up to 14-20 days a year. Usually, each term, a student is paired with an instructor and a few other students. Classes continue to be conducted online, with material due at set times. Most MFAs, whether low-res or full-res, require a thesis, and this is often what the student takes forward into the world as proof his investment was valid. The thesis may be a novel or book-length nonfiction project, a collection of short stories, a screenplay, or a chapbook of poetry.

MFAs are expensive and time-consuming and can leave you with a lot of debt, so this is not a decision to go into casually. Just how much debt? Tuition averages $7000 a semester for full residency MFAs at a public school and $19,000 a semester at a private school, which comes to between $28,000-74,000 for a two year program and $42,000-110,000 for a three year. Low residency programs are cheaper, averaging about $20,000-30,000 for overall tuition. Of course with travel expenses, this figure can go higher, since you have to either fly or drive to the school and then cover hotel and food costs while you're on campus.

In return for this significant outlay of money and time, there are two practical things that an MFA can do for you. It can help you get a teaching job. And finishing a thesis, at least in theory, makes it more likely you have something to take forward into the marketplace. Despite the fact that neither of these things are guaranteed to happen, the vast majority of the people I have spoken with don't regret getting their degree.

Here's my not-terribly-scientific experiment: I posted the question, "Was your MFA worth it?" on Facebook, and within an hour I had over fifty responses, which is an indication this is a hot button for a lot of people. Low-res MFAs especially are full of people in their thirties, forties, and fifties who perhaps feel guilty about the time they spent away from their spouses and kids, not to mention the dollars they ripped from the family budget. But even taking their possible guilt into account, it's still significant that of the over 100 MFA grads who ultimately responded to my "Was it worth it?" question, only one said "No." Quite a few noted that taking on educational debt at midlife was a bitter pill to swallow, with one woman noting, "I'll be paying off my student loan into eternity." But several people reported that they got teaching gigs courtesy of the degree, and a few more said they met their current agents either through programs at their MFAs or fellow grads. Seven said they got book deals.

In addition, an MFA offers certain intangibles — respondents noted it gave them "a great running start at a writer's life," "a chance to refine my craft," "endless contacts," and "increased self-respect." Applying to an MFA is like crossing a sort of internal Rubicon for many writers, a sign you're taking this writing thing seriously and are ready to covert a hobby or a vague hankering into a real career.

And besides, there are ways to do it without mortgaging the family farm. One graduate points out that a lot of MFA students are fully funded; in exchange for teaching Freshman comp at the university, she got a tuition waiver and a stipend. She believes that anyone who doesn't look for funding is foolish and adds that, "You can't put a price on the experience. Work that sucks can in fact become work that doesn't suck if you're open to the workshop process."

Chapter Four

What You Should Look for in an Agent and the Unexpected Things Agents Do

Agents are the gatekeepers of the publishing industry. If you hope to sell your novel to a large mainstream press for a hefty advance (or even a not-so-hefty advance) it's almost impossible to do this without an agent. Since agents only take on what they think they can sell — and since it's almost impossible to sell a novel to a large press without an agent — the judgment of an agent is often a self-fulfilling prophecy. If you can't convince an agent to represent you, odds are no editor will ever see, much less purchase, your manuscript.

Agents not only wield a lot of power, but they're also the only people who are 100% squarely in the writer's corner.

Don't get me wrong. Most editors are lovely people who were drawn into this line of work because they're passionate about books, and many authors develop real friendships with their editors. But the editor works for the publishing house and that will always be where her first loyalty lies. An editor might adore your book, but if she can acquire the manuscript for $10,000, there's absolutely no incentive for her to offer you $20,000. The agent, in contrast, gets a percentage of whatever you earn, so he has every incentive to try and get you more. Plus, in this topsy-turvy environment, in which publishing houses are constantly merging or folding and even the most seasoned editors fear for their jobs, the odds are that your longest lasting relationship will be with your agent. Writers and agents tend to bond for the long haul.

Finding and signing with an agent is the first major decision you'll make in the publishing process, and it can trigger huge, shuddering, junior-high-sized waves of anxiety. Starting with the fear that no one will want you at all.

Most writers desperately want to be able to say they have an agent. Not only is it a clear step on the path to publication, but having an agent is often seen as a stamp of legitimacy, a distinction that separates the pretenders from the contenders. If you sat down at a hotel bar in the middle of a writing conference and decided to slam a shot of tequila every time you heard a fellow writer say the words "my agent," you'd be drunk pretty fast. Beginning writers fall in love with those two quasi-magical words, and of course you want to be able to say them too. But don't let your eagerness lead you to the wrong agent. Because having the wrong agent is like having the wrong spouse — much worse than being on your own. Your goal should not simply be to find an agent but to find the right agent for you.

The right agent isn't just anyone who will sign you. Believe me. During my two-year hunt for an agent, I felt like some sort of desperate bridesmaid whose friends had all beaten her to the altar. Standards slip in that situation. You find yourself just trying to make eye contact with the last groomsman standing — or signing an incomprehensible contract with an agent whose business cards double as pizza fliers. The common wisdom is that writers don't choose agents, that agents choose writers and that any writer whose manuscript is plucked from the pile should be so damn grateful she shouldn't ask any questions. But you owe it to yourself to begin your search for an agent in as rational and self-aware a manner as possible. When you consider all the roles that agents play, it's clear why choosing the right one from the start can save you bucket loads of problems down the road.

What Do Agents Do?

Agents sell books

This is indeed the primary function of an agent, to present your book to an editor he thinks might buy it. Your agent's ability to successfully do this depends on three things: a) his understanding of your book and where it belongs in terms of a publisher, b) his knowledge about which editors are currently in the market and what they're looking for, and c) his general salesmanship, his ability to create excitement or buzz about your book.

When an agent agrees to represent you, he probably does so specifically because he already has some ideas about which editors would be a good match for your book. Agents and editors are people like anyone else, and they have relationships like anyone else, people they've worked with in the past and would either like to work with again or whom they know to avoid like the plague. If an agent and editor have already collaborated successfully, they'll probably both be eager to repeat that experience. Assuming they're a good fit in terms of genre and subject matter, the agent will bring that editor his new clients first, and the editor will be favorably disposed toward any new client that agent recommends. There's nothing particularly mysterious about the process. As in any other business, people gravitate towards people they click with and tend to work with them over and over.

If an agent knows several editors who might buy your book, how does he decide which one to approach first? This is where it gets a little tricky.

Books are sold in three ways. The first is the pre-empt. If an agent feels strongly that a certain editor is the best fit for a particular book, he might offer her an exclusive look for a limited period of time, usually a couple of weeks. If she indeed loves the book as much as the agent predicted, she'll offer a certain amount of money for an advance. If he in turn thinks it's a fair amount, then the sale is swiftly completed without any other editor ever having even looked at the manuscript. Writers tend to like these deals because they're fast, calm, don't involve any white-knuckle decisions, and their books end up with the editor their agent hand-selected as the perfect fit. Sometimes if the first editor on the list either passes or offers a small advance, the agent will then allow another editor at another house the chance to look at the book exclusively. But you still have only one editor reading and possibly bidding at any given time. Pre-empts usually bring in smaller advances but leave the agent and writer more in control of who ends up with the book.

The second method is the auction. The agent sends the book simultaneously to several editors and then, on a set date which is usually a few weeks in the future, an auction is held and the book goes to the highest bidder. This method is often used when a book is perceived as hot, i.e., potentially of interest to lots of editors, and the agent is trying to get the biggest advance possible. His goal is for a bidding war to break out, if say Random House offers $100,000, Little Brown counters with $150,000, Riverhead comes in at $165,000 and Random House ups the offer to $200,000. Writers love these deals because it's exciting to have people vie over your work and because auction fever can result in super-high advances. The downside is that you may end up with a house or an editor who is a slightly less-perfect fit than in the pre-empt model. But if your agent only invites certain hand-picked editors to bid at auction and figures that any of them would work, even that small drawback can be minimized.

The third way books get sold is what I call the Rocky method, i.e., the book just goes out there and takes hit after hit until something eventually goes right. Not all agents have the connections and clout to arrange pre-empts and auctions and not all books have the broad-based appeal to attract significant advances. In some cases, agents send books out for years before someone bites. Needless to say, these scenarios don't result in big advances from major publishers, but the writers are usually so worn down at this point, they'll happily take whatever is offered. Besides, just like in the movie, you occasionally hear of a book which, in true Rocky fashion, was rejected by everyone and languished for years and then winds up a bestseller.

No matter how the deal happens, the math works like this. The editor buys the book by offering an advance. (The term "advance" is short for "advance against royalties," and we'll discuss how this works later, in the contracts chapter.) Let's say your agent has taken the book to one of his favorite editors at Penguin, someone he's worked with many times before, and she offers $50,000. Happy day! You should do a little dance. For his trouble, your agent gets 15% of that advance and any subsequent royalties the book generates. (15% is definitely the going rate for legitimate agents, with 20% for subsidiary sales such as foreign rights and movies, so you should recoil from any agent who asks for more.) The advance is most often paid out in three installments: one upon signing, one upon the acceptance of the completed manuscript, and the final payment on the day the book is actually released for sale to the public.

So let's say you have a $50,000 deal with three equal payments due at signing, upon acceptance, and on publication day. You'll get a little over $16,000 upon signing. The check will be sent to your agent who will take out his 15% and forward the remainder to you, which is now down to about $14,000. On the day you get the check, be sure to send your agent a nice note of thanks.

In order to get you that money, he's demonstrated several different kinds of expertise. He's had to know what editor might buy your book. This knowledge is based on his history with a variety of different editors and what they like. He has lunch with these people. He's worked with them before. There is no way you could acquire that sort of relationship with an editor living in Seattle or Austin or Tampa or Duluth, sitting on your couch thumbing through your twenty-pound copy of *Writer's Marketplace*.

Even more importantly, he knew who had money to spend. Editors have budgets. Someone who has spent most of their money earlier in the year acquiring a few high profile books may not have the cash to bid on your book in November, even if they love it. But another editor, who hasn't acquired much lately, may have money left to spend and be favorably disposed to take on a new author. Again, there's no way you could know if an editor is tapped out or actively looking. And, even if through dumb luck you had managed to find the right editor at the right house at the right time and she had taken a look at your book, you would have had no idea if the advance she offered was a fair deal.

Which brings us to the second thing an agent does...

Agents advise

Publishing has always been a complex business — you're selling, after all, an intangible thing, an idea. This will never be the same as selling nuts and bolts, because an idea is worth precisely as much as people can convince each other it's worth. Not to mention that we're living in a time when, thanks to the advent of epublishing and the mergers of once-independent houses into large multimedia conglomerates, an already complex business is in a period of rapid change. The result is that even the most savvy writer probably won't know as much as an agent.

Another factor is that when the time comes to make decisions, you have to make them very quickly. Here's an example from my own story.

The mythic $50,000 offer I mentioned above wasn't mythic to me. The first eight editors that my agent David approached passed on my book. It felt like a complete kick in the gut at the time, but before I could mourn too severely, David was calling to report that he had shown the book to the second batch of eight editors on his list and that three of these had made an offer. They had all offered $50,000. At the time I thought it was odd that they had all offered the same amount, but since then I've realized that the first eight on the list were at the top precisely because they were editors who could make large offers without consulting anyone else and who could have, if necessary, entered into an auction. When they all passed and we moved on to the second batch, they were the second batch precisely because these were people who were authorized to offer around $50,000. Not a mega-advance, but certainly respectable.

Since they'd all offered the same amount, David urged me to talk to each of them by phone to see if I preferred one over another. I had great conversations with all three — these were heady days for me, folks — but I clicked especially well with an editor who wanted to bring the book out in paperback. David advised against going with her because he felt a paperback debut would damage my book's chances for foreign rights sales and certain high-level reviewers. I took his advice and went with one of the editors who was prepared to bring it out in hardback, and as it turns out, David was completely right. The foreign rights sales were very strong and I got reviewed in a couple of places that I doubt I would have scored with a paperback release.

So when an offer finally comes, it comes fast, with lots of bells and whistles attached. It's impossible to over-emphasize how confusing this period of time can be for a writer. I literally went from having no agent to having an agent and three editors bidding on the book within a six-week period. After years in which nothing (nothing!) happened, this felt like freefall. My background is journalism and finance. I've always prided myself on being able to figure out pretty much anything. I'm an independent person by nature who likes to make decisions swiftly and unilaterally. And on top of all that, I was a published nonfiction writer who had handled those contracts on her own for over twenty years. So, frankly, if I was lost, I think almost anyone would have been lost.

And as further info was flung at me — print runs, film rights, cover art, production schedules — I found myself time and time again turning to David for council. David is a gentle soul, the sort of man who would never ram his opinion down anyone's throat and who is terribly respectful of the writer's feelings. So it wasn't as if he ever bullied me into anything. Quite the contrary. I was the one begging for advice. I knew I was flying blind, and I hate to think how many times someone would have eaten my lunch if he hadn't been there to guide me through the process.

And after we'd chosen which editor to go with, David was also able to bump her up to $65,000 by allowing the publishing house to keep foreign rights. We'll talk more about how foreign rights can affect an author's bottom line later — they were a huge factor for me — but for now, just note that David was not only able to tell me what house would be best for the book, but to get them to sweeten the deal a little. What do you think the odds are I would have been able to do this on my own?

While every book and every deal is different and brings its own set of questions, I've heard lots of other writers talk about how much they needed their agents as advisors and sounding boards. Remember, your editor presumably likes you and your book…otherwise they wouldn't be standing there, cash in hand. But their goal is to get your book into their publishing house as cheaply as possible, so you can't count on them to tell you if you're getting screwed in terms of your subsidiary rights or the publicity budget. Writers sometimes bitch because agents are getting a piece of their action — but it's precisely because he's getting a piece of your action that your agent is motivated to watch your action carefully. He only makes money if you do.

Agents act as a buffer between the author and the editor after the book is sold

Even if you're at a great house and you love your editor, there are going to be rough patches along the way. I've talked to writers who were unhappy with their deadlines, revisions, cover art, publicity budgets, pretty much anything you can imagine. But when you're upset, it's never a good idea to call up your editor ranting and raving. After your fit of pique passes, you still have to work with this person.

Far better to sic your agent on him or her.

Now, agents have to work with these editors again too, especially if they're the sort of agents who sell over and over to the same houses. A smart agent won't want to ruin his relationship with an editor so he will be politic in his complaints. But he knows he doesn't have to work with that editor again immediately, or the next day, on matters as subtle and delicate as whether or not to kill off the heroine's mother in chapter two, so most agents will man up and take the hit of complaining on behalf of their authors.

One writer friend — whose book went through numerous rewrites, to the degree that her relationship with her editor was becoming increasingly acrimonious — says that her agent suggested she blame everything on him. Rather than saying, "I'm not sure about these changes," she would approach with, "My agent isn't sure about these changes." That way she could raise numerous objections without it ever seeming that she was contradicting her editor.

Agents also can take the hit for editors. A recent article in *Poets &Writers* magazine talked about all the things agents do behind the scenes and reminded readers how editors are afraid of losing their jobs. If one of the books under their charge isn't getting the in-house attention or budget it deserves, they may be reluctant to bring this up with the publisher. They're so nervous they don't want to rock the boat in-house by demanding more attention for their books and authors.

Enter the agent, who can question, demand, and complain with relative impunity. Once again, a smart agent knows he'll be working with these publishers again, so he doesn't go ballistic for the sheer hell of it, and he isn't rude or overly demanding. But he does recognize that he is less at the mercy of this publisher than the editor or the writer. So he will often be the logical one to ask, "What kind of publicity push are you planning for this book? Shouldn't we set a meeting to discuss it?"

Bottom line? Writers never have had any power and editors are losing theirs. Publishing houses are consolidating and there simply isn't enough time and money to go around. Sometimes agents are the only people who can successfully negotiate for a book within a house.

Agents edit

Here's one of the lesser known facts of contemporary publishing: in many cases, the editor and agent switch roles.

Before I sold my book I pictured an agent as a fast-talking guy in a suit, some combination of a carnival barker and a circa-1980s Gordon Gekko type, making deals while snorting lines of cocaine off a hooker's chest. The agent was all about getting the money — certainly no one you'd want to hang around with and the last person on earth you'd turn to for advice on how to improve your book. The editor, probably a thin, earnest young woman from a Seven Sisters school with a profound knowledge of Yeats and Woolf, would be the person who would go through the manuscript with you line by line, debating the placement of a comma or sharing long dreamy conversations about symbolism and syntax.

Boy was I wrong. As it turns out, at least in my case, my agent was the one who helped me edit the book and my editor then took it pretty much intact. At her suggestion, I added one small scene, but her main function, ironically, was to sell the book within the house — to get the salespeople, foreign rights team, publicity department, etc. excited enough about my book to give it some attention and a chunk of the budget. And since then I've heard of similar experiences from other writers.

What's the reason for this role switch? I think there are several. As publishing houses merged and magazines collapsed, a lot of editors lost their jobs and a fair chunk of them went into agenting. Even some of those who weren't forcibly displaced noticed that there was more money to be made on the agenting side of the fence. The result is a fresh young platoon of agents with editorial backgrounds who are more than qualified to serve as their clients' first readers. These editor-turned-agents know that the better shape they can get a manuscript in, the more likely it is to attract a buyer, so there's a monetary motivation behind their willingness to step into this editorial role — and besides, I think for a lot of them it just comes automatically. In their hearts, they're still editors.

Another reason for the flip-flop is that in the age of the gigantic media house, it's harder than it's ever been for a book to get attention, even after it's sold, and even from the people who bought it. Grand Central, for example, is a medium-sized imprint and it releases about 30 books each season. Even that many releases can stretch budgets and editorial time to the breaking point, but then you factor in that Grand Central's parent company, Hachette, owns not just them, but several other publishers including Little Brown and Warner Books. A big house has lots of mouths to feed and some little books starve.

This is precisely why writers aim to work with managing editors or those who have their own imprints, those editors at the top of the heap who don't have to answer to anyone. The downside of this plan is that the higher up the power pyramid an editor has climbed, the less time she's going to have to work with you, especially if you're an unproven, first time author. After the big strong editor signs you, the actual editing of your book will probably be farmed out to an underling. Or worse, since job turnover is rampant among junior editors, most of whom are living on poverty-level wages and commuting in from cramped apartments in the less fashionable neighborhoods of Brooklyn, your book may be edited by a whole series of underlings, each of whom suggests complicated changes and then disappears. In short, a hyper-powerful editor sometimes turns out to be an absentee editor.

But there are also major advantages to a powerful editor. The first is that she can, if so inclined, write a big check. The second is that big editors tend to have big egos and they don't like to see books they've acquired sink into oblivion. So they are often prepared to throw the full weight of their position behind the books they've personally given the nod to. A powerful editor means your book is more likely to be positioned well within the house.

Smart agents know all this, which is one of the reasons they step into the editorial role when necessary. Not only will a well-edited manuscript fetch a higher price in the marketplace, but if the manuscript comes through the door just about perfect, the agent has also saved the writer the nightmare of being edited by a revolving door series of junior editors.

Does this always happen? Of course not. In the world of publishing the two most useless words are "always" and "never." I know authors whose editors served as just that, editors, working through the manuscript with them line by line. But the new paradigm is that manuscripts, at least those by first-time writers, are arriving at their publishing houses in pristine condition, courtesy of a lot of preliminary work between the author and agent. So be prepared for the fact that your agent is not only a salesperson, legal advisor, advocate and buffer, but he may be your first editor as well.

THERE ARE MANY VARIETIES OF AGENTS

The Power Agent

The power agent is all about showing you the money. If you subscribe to *Publisher's Marketplace*, it isn't hard to pick these people out. They're the ones doing "major" or "significant" deals, meaning advances in the $200,000 plus range. These agents usually either work with big agencies or head their own.

The advantages? The possibility of major cash from a major house and, for this reason, very few authors who get the chance to work with a power agent say no. Since a large advance means the publisher will be trying to protect that investment, power agents are often successful at getting big publicity budgets for their authors. TV appearances, book tours, positioning in chain bookstores, and a better-than-average shot at reaching the best-seller list, these are the kind of perks that can come with being the client of a power agent.

The disadvantages? After the ink is dry on the contract, these guys won't hold your hand through the rest of the process. One of my friends got a blockbuster-esque advance for her first book and her agent then disappeared. He wasn't there for the follow up because he's the sort of guy who moves swiftly from one deal to the next. Due to the size of her check, she was okay with it, and learned to direct her questions to his assistant. And if you're not one of the agent's star clients, you'll get even less attention than that. Another writer, who has sold four books without having breakout success, reports that his high-profile agent "probably wouldn't recognize me if she passed me on the street." And of course, having a power agent is no guarantee of a major deal, or even that he'll sell your book at all. No agent has a perfect track record.

The Editorial Agent

The editorial agent usually comes from, you guessed it, an editorial background, and specializes in getting books in tip-top shape for the marketplace. Authors may work with these agents for months before the books are sent to editors. An editorial agent can help you flesh out a nonfiction proposal, develop a high-concept idea, or turn a bloated novel into a lean, mean, award-winning machine. Some of these books go on to big advances and some don't. An editorial agent might feel just as gratified by representing a book that wins a literary prize or in helping a talented writer reach a new level of artistry.

The advantage? Editorial agents can be instrumental in helping you elevate the craft of your book and that may be what you need most. They also tend to care deeply about the books they represent and there are many joys to be found in this type of collaboration.

The disadvantage? Most of the time, these agents will only take on projects that speak to them personally. This is a subjective decision, so it's hard to say which authors they'll be drawn to and which they won't. Editorial agents are also a bad bet for anyone in a rush. These cycles of rewrites can take years.

The Parental Agent

Some agencies describe themselves as "one stop" or "full service," and the agents within, especially if they also happen to be owners of the agency, tend to involve themselves in every aspect of an author's career. Parental agents are like editorial agents in that they become quite involved with the writers in their care...but, unlike editorial agents, parental agents will often take on less-literary work. In fact, many of them specialize in genre fiction and how-to nonfiction and like to work with writers who produce multiple projects quickly. They're in it for the duration, and may talk more about your long-term career than whatever book happens to be in their hands at the moment.

The advantage? If you just want to write and not think about the financial part of the game, this type of agent can hold a lot of appeal. In fact, many of these agents openly claim that their job is to shield the writer from the more unsavory aspects of the publishing process. And because of their commitment to the long-term career and not just the project of the moment, parental agents are also the least likely to sever ties with a client, even if their books don't sell.

The disadvantage? "Parental" is a double-edged sword and these agents may shield you so effectively that they keep you in the dark. One of my friends had experienced moderate success in the YA market but always yearned to write adult novels as well. When she showed her mainstream novel to her agent, complete with a couple of mild sex scenes, he announced he "wouldn't let her ruin her career" by bringing out a book that was so much in contrast with her established YA platform. It wasn't until she heard herself say the sentence, "I've got to figure out a way to talk him into it," that she realized their relationship had devolved into a weird sort of daughter-daddy dynamic where she was seeking permission to write the books she wanted to write. She ultimately left that agent and is happily working with another, who not only sold her mainstream adult novel but treats her as more of an equal in the decision making.

The Newbie Agent

The newbie is that bright-eyed creature you meet at a pitch conference or who's featured in a *Writer's Digest* magazine article titled something like, "These Agents are Seeking YOUR Work." The fact they're openly looking for clients is proof they're new to the game. They generally work for established agencies and are often presently the assistants of more experienced agents, but eager to develop their own client lists on the side.

The advantages? Like the article says, they're looking for you. The newbie is generally the easiest kind of agent to find and sign with. If they are indeed the protégé of an established agent, their inexperience isn't that much of a problem, since presumably they have mentors to guide them through the process. In fact, one nonfiction writer I know is very happy with the young woman who not only signed him, but helped him whip his travel memoir proposal into market-ready shape. "She only had three clients when I signed, so she gave me all the attention I needed," he says. "And when it was time to sell the book, she had the clout of her whole agency behind her. A new agent who works at an old agency can be the best of both worlds."

The disadvantages? Since they haven't worked with editors before, newbies rarely have the personal relationships that lead to quick sales, nor do they have the reputation to draw lots of bidders to an auction. Thus, advances with a newbie agent tend to be lower. Their inexperience can also be problematic when it comes to contract negotiation or playing hardball once the book is sold. "I was the first significant deal my agent ever did," says one writer, "and later he admitted he was learning as he went. It worked out okay, but I'm glad I didn't know just how green he was during all those months I was relying on his advice."

The Businesslike Agent

Some agents exist solely to advise their clients on details of the deal. They usually come into the process after the writer and editor have already met and agreed on the basics. In other words, while the agent's job is usually to get the manuscript ready and then connect the writer to the best editor of the project, the businesslike agent does neither of these things. He comes in at the end, to make sure the writer's rights are being protected in the contract.

Businesslike agents might be solicited by the writer. Perhaps he's won a literary contest, where publication is part of the prize. Or perhaps the writer's a celebrity or is sitting on a timely, blockbuster concept — he was the only survivor of a well-publicized plane crash, she was famously dumped by her husband, who then ran off with a movie star, he's the reigning Super Bowl MVP who's just announced he's battling a drug problem. In other words, there's an idea but not a book, and an editor is willing to work with the "writer," even to the point of bringing in a ghost writer. The contest winner or celeb might seek a businesslike agent in this situation just to make sure he's getting the best deal possible.

Just as often, though, it's the editor who suggests the businesslike agent enter the process. Some editors won't work with unagented authors, even if they've approached these authors themselves. Bringing in an agent is the editorial equivalent of reading the writer his Miranda rights — insurance that the writer won't later show up with complaints or even with a lawsuit claiming he wasn't adequately represented in the negotiations.

The advantages? Obviously these agents aren't hard to find, since the deal is already in place. They parachute in, work on the contract, and parachute out — and that may be all you need them to do.

The disadvantages? This is a very limited relationship and in fact you may never even meet this sort of agent face to face. If you have fantasies of a cozier author-agent relationship, they won't be realized. Of course, in these situations, the primary relationship is between the writer and the editor so you may not need to feel connected to your agent. Also, because businesslike agents do relatively little in contrast to other types of agents, writers may resent giving them the full 15% cut of not only the advance, but any subsequent royalties. Some agents offer a discount if they merely advise on a pre-existing deal, and it's also possible that an attorney with expertise in intellectual property law can serve the same advisory function for a one-time fee.

The Faux Agent

We've described these people before but it bears repeating. Not everyone who claims to be an agent is really in the game, and sometimes the big-talkers aren't doing deals.

All it really takes for someone to become an agent is a trip to Kinko's. There are no established qualifications — no license, no certification, no degree, no test. Run a few business cards and you're in business. And if you walked through the halls of a writer's conference with your Kinko's business cards you'd have a roster of potential clients within minutes.

So what motivates these faux agents? If they aren't making money by selling books, why do they pretend to be agents?

Part of it may be ego. Some of these people have other jobs that support them, generous spouses, or trust funds; since they aren't looking to publishing for a living, they're free to flit around the edges of the publishing industry, enjoying the attention they get at conferences and the fawning devotion of their clients.

Or perhaps it's profit. There are all kinds of ways that people can make money off of writers that have nothing to do with selling books. Faux agents may be getting paid merely to show up at these conferences. They may be charging fees to read the manuscripts that are submitted to them. They may be suggesting their clients need book doctors and then receive a kickback for those referrals. Or they may be shills for vanity publishers, who look to these faux agents to send them a steady stream of customers.

The problem is that it can be tough to recognize a faux agent. They don't lurk around like pedophiles outside the school yard or like the guy selling fake Rolexes on the corner. If you're beginning to get the uneasy feeling, you may have been swooped up by a faux agent, trust those instincts and do some research. Start by looking for these red flags:

1. The agent requests a fee to read your manuscript or requires any sort of retainer up front.

2. The agent tries to refer you to another service that charges fees. If the agent immediately directs you to a book doctor, management service, website designer, or vanity publisher, that's a very bad sign. He may be living totally off paid referrals or he may even be part owner in the company he's steering you toward.

3. Complaints have been lodged against him. Writers aren't exactly known for suffering in silence, so the odds are if an agent has shafted a fair number of writers, there's a record of it. The Science Fiction and Fantasy Writers of America (SFWA) hosts a site called Writer Beware (www.writerbeware.com) that's useful for writers of any genre. Among the information found there are lists of agents, publishers, and scams to avoid. Another site, Predators and Editors (www.pred-ed.com) offers, among other information, a list of agents which notes if they charge fees or if any lawsuits have been launched against them. It's important to remember that not all writer complaints bear equal weight; if about 70% of the books agents take on sell, that means that almost a third of them don't, and this results in lots of disgruntled writers. Simply failing to sell a certain project doesn't mean someone is a bad agent — especially if the record shows this agent has had success selling other books. Which leads us to…

4. He or she has no track record of sales on *Publisher's Marketplace* (www.publishersmarketplace.com).

5. The agent is not affiliated with AAR (www.aaronline.org). Again, not all agents are members of the Association of Authors' Representatives, but membership is one sign of how serious the agent is.

6. When you ask for referrals, the agent either demurs or directs you towards "clients" who have either not yet sold their books or who have, on the agent's advice, self-published. When they refer

to deals that are "pending" or projects that have generated "a lot of interest," that just means nothing has yet sold. Successful agents display the books they've represented on their websites and are happy to introduce you to their published authors.

7. Agenting is not their primary source of income. If this is a part-time job, they're either a beginner or just playing at it.

8. His correspondence with you is full of typos and bad grammar. This is not an industry that forgives such lapses, and if the agent cannot represent you in a professional way, he's worse than useless. One writer I know, whose agent had been submitting her book for a year without success, finally asked to see the letter he was sending to editors. She was horrified when it looked as if it had been written by one of her middle school students. "No wonder no editor wanted to see my book," she says. "This was clearly amateur hour."

9. The agent is extremely enthusiastic or extremely self-assured but short on specifics. If you ask what editors he or she is planning to approach, or at a later date request a list of editors who have been approached, this information should be provided to you in a clear, direct manner. The best agents have nothing to hide.

Beginning the Agent Search

The first thing you need is an agent wish list. In terms of books, both the general *Writer's Marketplace* and the more focused *Guide to Literary Agents* are good starting places. The listings give you a general idea of what that agent is looking for and how open he or she is to new clients. If you prefer to search on line, there are many sites that list agents, such as www.agentquery.com.

You'll come away with a staggeringly large list of possibilities, so the next step is to divide this list into categories, A for your dream agents, B for ones you'd be proud to work with, C for agents who are just starting out but are otherwise promising, and so on. You can zero in on your A list by:

1. Looking at the acknowledgement pages in books written by

authors you admire. Writers invariably thank their agents in these pages.

2. Searching www.publishersmarketplace.com, using both the Who Represents Whom function and a general search of who is doing the most deals in your genre.

3. Any agent you have a personal connection with — they represent a friend, you've met them at a conference, etc. — should also go on the A list.

I'd say you need at least twelve agents on this A list. If anyone comes close — perhaps you met her at a conference, but you weren't that impressed or she represents an author you like but doesn't seem to do a lot of deals — move that name down to your B or C list. With luck, you won't have to go to those lists, but it never hurts to have lots of options at the ready. You don't want to have the feeling that your future depends on the judgment of only a handful of people. A nice fat agent wish list can keep you from overreacting if and when the rejections come rolling in.

Oh, and just to state the obvious, your agent should never know that he was on your C list and the last person you vowed to try before you heaved your book into the Atlantic. Or maybe it's not so obvious. I once heard an author accepting an award thank her agent in such an incredibly ungracious way that it was clear he hadn't been her first choice. Once you sign with an agent, it's probably best you make a bonfire with your lists — and, by the same token, editors should never know if they weren't your first choice either.

When you've got your list sorted out, stand back and ask yourself a few questions. Depending on their answers you may move a few agents up or down.

Am I choosing this agent because he or she is truly the best fit for this project or am I instead shopping for a brand-name agent? If you're a mystery novelist with a recurring character who is looking for a multi-book deal, your ideal agent is someone who has relationships with editors at houses that publish mystery series. You might want the ego rush of snagging a star agent who represents the current Pulitzer Prize winner, but if that agent is inexperienced with mysteries, all that glamour is pretty meaningless.

What functions do I need my agent to serve? Some writers have already found their publishers and simply need an agent to look over the contract and advise them on rights. Some writers have a killer idea but know they need editorial help to bring their writing to the same level as their concept. Maybe you see the writer-agent relationship as a creative partnership and maybe you just want him to show you the money then get the heck out of Dodge. It's possible to get any of these things, but only if you go in with a clear idea of what you're seeking, and if you understand that, just as there is no perfect deal, there is no perfect agent. Obviously, it's hard to tell much about an agent from just looking at a list but some basic research might give you more clues. Some agents have blogs and many writers have blogs in which they talk about their agents. Even looking over the list of books the agent has represented over the past few years should give you some idea of where his strengths lie.

Do I understand that this is only the first step? Perhaps because it's so tough to get an agent, writers often indulge the fantasy that agents are miracle workers, capable of snapping their fingers and transporting the writer to the best-seller list. Getting an agent is an important first step in selling your book, but it's not a guarantee that the book will sell or sell well.

Am I prepared to treat this as a professional relationship and not the answer to all my problems? Agents hate working with clients who expect too much, or who change from grateful to demanding a nanosecond after signing the contract. Your goal should be a friendly professional relationship with a person whose opinion you respect and whose judgment you trust. But never forget that, even after you have an agent and a publisher, a publicist and a copy editor, and maybe even a cabana boy, the ultimate responsibility for your work and your career will always lie with you.

QUICK QUIZ: DO YOU NEED AN AGENT?

The answer is "Yes" if any of these things apply:

— You're looking for an advance. An advance, short for "advance against royalties," is the amount of money you get from a publisher before the book comes out and publishers rarely pay significant upfront money to unagented authors.

— You want a big-six publisher. The big six are Random House, Simon & Schuster, HarperCollins, Hachette Book Group, Georg Von Holtzbrinck, and Penguin. Following all the recent mergers in the publishing industry these six and their subsidiaries pretty much are mainstream New York publishing. Workman, who owns four independent imprints, including the prestigious Algonquin, also deals primarily with agented material.

— You have a high-concept nonfiction idea that needs developing. If you're working off a book proposal, your material is especially time-sensitive, or has blockbuster potential, you'll need an agent to not only help you flesh out the concept but also to get you enough of an advance to live on while you finish the book.

— Anyone has approached you about your book. This may sound a little odd, since it seems like if you already have an editor or publisher who's interested, you can bypass getting an agent. But if someone approaches you, that's all the more reason you'll need unbiased council as you negotiate the contract and advance. The good news is, if you have an offer in hand, it's usually easy to get an agent.

You don't need an agent if:

— You write poetry or literary short stories (unless you are also working on a novel or memoir).

— You'd prefer to be published by a small independent or university press.

— You have a self-explanatory or how-to style nonfiction project. I have successfully updated my travel guide *Walt Disney*

World with Kids for twenty-two years without an agent. Many nonfiction books are unagented, and if a reader can tell by the title whether or not he needs your book — as in my case, where you're either going to Disney World with kids or you aren't — so can an editor.

— You want to keep all elements of your publishing experience under your own control. If you consider your book an entrepreneurial project, you may prefer to self-publish and keep a bigger percentage of each book you sell.

Chapter Five

How to Get an Agent in 384 Easy Steps

It would seem that finding an agent is a fairly straightforward process, but for most writers it's neither direct nor easy. Here's my particular story.

My friends Dawn and Alison had not only preceded me into publication, but they had both gotten large advances from well-respected publishers. Despite their success, or maybe because of it, I became more determined than ever to make it on my own. So I stupidly, stupidly, stupidly declined their offers to introduce me to their agents. Did I mention this was stupid? Because of this decision, I threw away two years of my life on an emotionally draining and fruitless search for literary representation.

Well, that might be a tad melodramatic. As we'll see repeatedly through this book, every decision has a flip side and nothing that happens to you in the publishing world is either 100% good or bad. The downtime allowed me to further polish my manuscript, which turned out to be a very good thing. It confirmed just how hard it can be to find an agent, which made me appreciate the fine agent I ended up with even more. Most importantly, these two years taught me a crucial lesson: publishing is a business of relationships. While we'd all been working on our novels, my friends had helped me in the writing process, so I'm not sure why I was so reluctant to let them help me similarly in the publication process. Probably just a natural human reluctance to seem like I was using my friends and my acute awareness that, at least at that point in time, I had nothing to offer them in return.

So instead I bought a big heavy *Writer's Market* and started working my way through the list of agents in the back. I figured those whose names started with an "A" got the most queries — one shudders to think how many hopefuls poor Nicole Arangi encounters in a year — and that maybe a lot of people used reverse psychology and started at the back of the alphabet. So I began in the middle, with the Ms, and starting querying. My system for prioritizing my query list wasn't very scientific. I was doing things like querying agents who shared my initials or who had the same surname as my first boyfriend.

I made a lot of mistakes with this approach. First and foremost, I didn't have a strong query letter. At the time I thought it was pretty good, perhaps because as a freelance magazine writer, I'd written so many queries that I had the nonfiction pitch down to a science. But describing a nonfiction idea is a snap compared to describing a novel, not to mention the fact it is always easier to describe what you want to do than it is to summarize what you've just done. Pitch-and-sell conferences didn't exist back then, and my description of the novel was rather vague. Not enough to entice a busy agent to request a full manuscript.

Another mistake? Initials aside, I didn't have any particular reason to believe any of these agents were a good fit for my book. I'd done virtually no research into who they represented or what editors they'd worked with in the past. Their *Writer's Digest* descriptions said they handled literary and mainstream fiction and that was good enough for me.

And finally, blind querying is a statistically unlikely way to find an agent. The most likely way is the option I'd passed on, an introduction from a writer friend.

I didn't make it all the way through the alphabet. After forty-something rejections, I broke down and asked Dawn and Alison for help.

Within a month, Dawn's agent had passed and Alison's had said yes.

At the time I was pretty embarrassed about this, like I was the ugly cousin the popular girl had to set up on a date. I couldn't shake the feeling that David had taken me on as a favor to a valued client. Let me be clear. David never did anything to make me feel this way. He has always treated me with respect. Alison never did anything to make me feel this way. She herself, in fact, had met David through a friend's introduction. My paranoia was entirely self-induced. I couldn't stop indulging the foolish fantasy that if you're terribly clever and you write a good enough book, there's some way to make it through the publication process on sheer merit, without heaping tablespoons of friendship, luck, and hustle helping you along the way.

I'm over that now.

I eventually realized that, while an introduction from a fellow writer is the most statistically likely way of acquiring an agent, it's still not statistically likely. Alison has introduced several writers to David over the years and I'm the only one he's signed. Since then I've recommended five people and he hasn't taken on any of them either. When a writer friend asks his or her agent to take a look at your work — something that most writers will only do if they believe in you strongly, since no writer wants to damage their own relationship with their agent by sending him crap — all that friend has bought you is a good reading by that agent. This in itself is a great gift. Agents get a lot of queries and very rarely ask to see the full manuscript. So if your friend gets an agent to actually read your book you should take that friend to lunch. Or maybe give him a kidney. He's gotten you farther than you likely would have gotten on your own. But an introduction isn't a guarantee that an agent will sign you as a client.

Since I couldn't grasp that David believed in my book, I didn't fully celebrate. I kept calling David "Alison's agent" instead of "my agent."

Why was I being such a dweeb? Because I couldn't get past the fact that even though the ball was finally rolling, it wasn't rolling in the way I'd expected. I didn't feel the way I thought I'd feel.

Every step in the road to publication is tinged with a sense of "Yes, but..." Things never seem to unfold exactly as you thought they would, and even victories come at a price. Eventually you get to the point where you let go of the fantasy of how it should happen and learn to relish the moments when anything happens at all, but I wasn't there yet. I even blogged about feeling like a literary imposter and, to my great shock, I got an email from David, coolly reminding me that he sees hundreds of manuscripts and he never would have taken on my book unless he liked it. I deserved the smack down, even though my first thought was, "Why on earth is Alison's agent reading my blog?"

Everyone in publishing is connected to everyone else, through more complex means than any of us can ever understand. I had written the post because I was trying to explore the reality that, even after getting what I'd been saying I wanted for years, i.e., an agent, I still had the same self-doubts. But in the process of indulging my own insecurities, I'd been unprofessional and risked hurting David's feelings. Everything you put out in this world eventually comes back to you — sometimes indirectly, through the web of hearsay and gossip, and sometimes with the speed and power of a boomerang. So I learned this lesson the hard way: Think before you speak. Think long and hard before you write.

Now that David was my agent — Yay? Yay! — I wanted us to actually meet. I planned a mid-November trip to New York so that he, Alison, and I could all sit down over dinner. The years of querying had convinced me that nothing moved fast in this world — that, in fact, documents scraped through the system with glacier-like speed and any agent who responded to a writer within two months could be honestly praised as a fast reactor. David had sent me what I would later learn was a pretty standard contract — we'll talk more about contracts in Chapter 7 — and I'd passed it along to an attorney I was dating for a once-over. Again, I was thinking we had plenty of time. But when I told David I'd bring the contract to our meeting in two weeks, he said fine, but in the meantime he was going to start showing the manuscript to editors.

This surprised me. Why would he start trying to sell my book when I hadn't yet signed the contract? With Thanksgiving, Christmas, and the end of the year looming, what was the rush? We hadn't even discussed edits. Wouldn't it make more sense to sit on things until January, after we'd met, made any necessary changes, formalized the deal? By then editors would have returned to their desks after the holidays in a "new year, new projects" frame of mind.

But, as it turns out, David's eagerness to get the wheels rolling was a very good sign. All those months I'd spent looking for an agent had given me more than enough time to get the manuscript in great shape so I didn't need a line edit. Furthermore, contracts between agents and writers are a bit of a formality — some agents don't bother with them at all. These relationships can be terminated by either party at any time without much legal explanation or recourse. If leaving a publisher is a bit like a divorce — you can certainly sever ties but not without legal and financial fallout — leaving an agent is more like breaking up with a boyfriend or girlfriend. You might be emotionally devastated, but there's not a lot of paperwork. Since the agent-writer connection is primarily a verbal agreement, David felt quite comfortable acting as my agent before he had, at least in terms of a contract, become my agent.

But most importantly, he knew that November and December could be an excellent time to sell my book. Anyone who hadn't spent all their money for the year might be in the mood to make a last-minute deal.

"What's the rush?" my lawyer-boyfriend kept saying, but I knew David had done a great job for Alison and I wanted to be able to hand him the contract at our meeting. I signed on the bottom line, threw the document in my purse, and hopped on the plane. This was going to be glamorous, right? At long last I was heading to

New York to meet my agent. I told the guy in the plane seat beside me all about it and, when he pretended to be asleep, I told the lady on the other side.

Both Alison and David live in Brooklyn so we agreed to meet at a little Tuscan restaurant between their neighborhoods.

David was nothing like I expected. (Are you sensing a developing theme here? Nothing in publishing is ever like you expect.) I imagined New York literary agents to be hard-driving and fast-talking, but David was wearing a sweater vest and carrying a canvas bag weighted down with an 800-page biography of John Cheever. We sat at a tiny little table, knees to knees, and, before we'd even put in our drink order, he informed me that he had shown my book to eight editors and they had all said no.

Alison later told me that she'd been afraid I was going to faint. Apparently all the color drained out of my face. The waiter showed up, thank God, so I had a couple of moments to try and pull myself together. Alison and David both ordered rabbit. I'd had pet rabbits as a child, which in my classically nerdy, destined-to-be-a-writer way, I'd named after historical figures. Since then I've never been able to accept the idea of eating a little Magellan or Cleopatra. I glanced at the menu and said I wanted minestrone. This evening marked the first and probably last time in my life that I've been unable to eat. I couldn't seem to get my mind around the fact that in a mere two weeks eight editors had read my book. This doubled the number of people who had ever read my book. The fact they had all additionally passed on it was too much to even absorb. I was sure that David had agreed to meet us here out of a gentlemanly desire to dump me in person, to feed me a bowl of minestrone and then release me into the desperate streets of Brooklyn.

Despite the darkness of the room, David must have noticed the same thing Alison had, i.e., that I was on the verge of a swoon. He pawed through his knapsack and pulled out a crumpled sheet of paper. On it was a list of sixteen names with the top eight crossed out. He explained that while the first eight names of the list had indeed passed, he was now going to send the book out to the next eight names on the list.

And then he explained why, out of the hundreds of editors in New York, he had chosen those sixteen.

He went down the list one at a time, discussing authors these editors had worked with, other writers whose books were in some way similar to mine. Or he explained why he suspected that so-and-so might still have money to spend in the waning weeks of the year or why their house might be a suitable home for my book. The rabbits arrived at some point, lying naked and accusatory across David and Alison's plates, and I may have made a half-hearted attempt to spoon a little minestrone past my numb lips. I managed to say, "Do you want the contract?" and he said, "Well, yeah," with some confusion, since that was ostensibly the point of this meeting in the first place. It began to dawn on me that my career, while not exactly off to a blazing start, was not entirely over either. I'd like to say I rallied all at once, but I didn't. This night will forever remain frozen in my mind as The Silence of the Rabbits.

As we awkwardly shook hands and headed off in our separate directions, I was still in so much shock that Alison linked her arm through mine just to keep me from stepping in front of a cab. Once we got back to her apartment, I lay down on the couch, fully dressed with my shoes on, and she covered me with an afghan. I stayed there for the next two days. Periodically, I would lift my head and ask, "Is he going to dump me?" and she would say, "Of course not." Her friends, most of them also writers, dropped in to pay their respects. They would stand beside the couch, gaze sadly down at my limp form, and talk about me as if I were not only the author of an unsalable manuscript, but also deaf.

I went home the day before Thanksgiving and by the first week of December three editors out of the second wave of eight had made an offer on the book. When you're tempted to shake me for being such a ninny, remember that I'd gone from someone without an agent to someone with three potential editors within a matter of six weeks. People think that when writers finally get agents and sell their books, they're happy — and you are, but in sort of a numbed out, drank-too-much-cough-syrup, dreamlike way. It can be hard to ask the right questions, or to enter into the conversations swirling around you in any kind of meaningful manner.

When David pulled out his crumpled piece of paper, I had no idea how lucky I was. I had an agent with a plan. The one question writers need to ask prospective agents is, "Who are you going to show my book to, and why?" and the agents need to provide some version of what David gave me, i.e., a systematic explanation of why these editors would be a good fit for the book. I didn't know to ask this of David — he just offered it up on his own.

This is one of the major reasons you need to choose your agent carefully and make sure she or he is someone you completely trust. When you're on the outside of the circle, trying to get an agent or sell a book, it feels like nothing ever happens, but once you're on the inside of the circle, things happen freakishly fast and the experience is utterly disorienting. Being a writer is like being a cop — long stretches of boredom punctuated by moments of sheer terror. So it's not enough to have an agent, that agent has to be someone whose advice you can take on the fly — not just during the selling process, but during everything that comes after.

Four Ways to Get an Agent

Ask to be Introduced

Your best bet, by far, is to be recommended to the agent by a friend or teacher. Some agents build their client list solely through referrals, and if someone they know is willing to vouch for you, they may even ask for your manuscript in its entirety. This doesn't mean they'll finish it, or that they'll take you on as a client, but it's far better than the usual system, where the agent only requests a handful of pages.

As we've discussed before, an introduction isn't a slam-dunk, but even if the agent takes a pass on your book, he or she is more likely to write you a polite letter and perhaps offer some general feedback. Even if the answer is no, thank the agent for his or her time and thank your friend for the recommendation.

And then move on. One of the main advantages of the network building we've discussed in previous chapters is that it will lead you to lots of friends with agents, and if one recommendation doesn't work out, perhaps another one will.

Meet the Agent Face to Face

Agents sometimes appear at conferences looking for clients, and this can be a great way to get your foot in the door. Conferences connected to schools and MFA programs are almost always legit, and while pitch conferences, as we've discussed, are a little iffier, they still have possibilities.

What will usually happen at these conferences is that if the agent likes your basic pitch or idea, he or she will ask to see more. Sometimes a few pages, sometimes a few chapters, sometimes the entire manuscript. Send what they request as fast as you can, along with a cover letter reminding the agent when and how you met.

Win a Contest or Get Published in a Respected Lit Magazine

Some agents look for new talent through literary magazines, writing contests, or anthologies. Obviously it's a rush to have an agent contact you, but don't be so flattered that you let your normal precautions lapse. Before you submit a book-length manuscript, much less sign a contract, do the normal research you would do before querying.

Query

And then there's the humble query letter. In the last chapter we discussed how to create an agent wish list and, if you have no published friends to introduce you, have never won a contest or met an agent at a conference, sometimes the only route open to you is to approach agents by letter and email.

A query is just what it sounds like — a question — and the question in this case is, "Would you like to represent this book?" The tone of a query is a bit like a jacket copy on a novel; it should give the recipient just enough information to make them want to keep reading, but not so much that they feel like they've already read the whole book.

It's no secret that blind querying is a long shot. The official industry estimate is that "fewer than 1% of queries result in deals," and it's actually far fewer. One agent told me she gets 250 queries a month and has taken on two new clients in the past year, which would come down to more like .0006 percent. But you still meet writers all the time who say they got their agents through this method. The trick seems to be to simultaneously follow the rules and stand out.

Some agents accept only query letters, while others like a sample chapter or a few pages attached as well. Most accept email queries while a few stick with snail mail. Go to their individual websites, click on submission guidelines, and then do exactly what they say to do. This isn't tenth-grade history; if an agent asks for five pages you don't get bonus points for sending a 300-page manuscript. In fact, all you'll get is your query promptly bounced right back to you.

Also, scrutinize their websites to make absolutely sure you're sending your query to an agent who represents books like yours. Nothing infuriates an agent like getting a query about a collection of short stories when she has clearly stated that she only handles nonfiction. Sounds simple, but agents report that there are still writers who go into a sort of querying frenzy, sending out mass-produced queries to everyone on their list with no regard to what the agent has said she's seeking. You shouldn't be surprised to get a form rejection letter when you've sent out a preprinted query letter.

Querying several agents at once doesn't mean you send them all the same query. If you've done your research, you have enough information on each agent to tweak your query to suit their particular interests, or at least to personalize the first paragraph.

Also, even though you may have lots of ideas and ten different projects in the works, develop a separate query for each book. Agents aren't looking for a one-book wonder, so it's good to have a long-term plan that includes lots of books, but if you try to pitch multiple ideas in one query it will become too long and too muddled. You might refer briefly to other projects near the end of your letter or mention if the book you've just pitched is part of a projected series, but keep the majority of the query crisp and focused on the project at hand.

QUERY LETTER FORMAT

The ideal query letter sticks to one page and follows this basic formula:

Paragraph one: State the name and genre of your book and tell the agent that you're seeking representation. This is also the place to explain (or to remind the agent) why you're chosen her — you met at a conference, you have a mutual friend, or he represents an author you admire. Agents like to know that you're a fan of one of their authors and that you've researched their agency, but keep the flattery to a minimum and — above all — be honest. One agent reports that she got a query from a writer gushing about how much he loved a certain book by one of her writers. There was just one little problem. The book he claimed to adore hadn't been published yet. "He must have read about the deal in *Publisher's Marketplace*," she says. "If someone lies to you in the first paragraph, there's no way you'd work with him."

Paragraph two: Give the elevator pitch for your book, a two or three line description of the project. Summarizing a whole book in a single paragraph is never easy to do, so practice your pitch on friends or run it by your critique group. If you want to compare your work to other writers, make sure the comparisons are apt.

Don't just fling out the names of best-sellers at random or merge two bizarrely unlikely writers such as "in the style of Flannery O'Connor and Dan Brown."

Paragraph three: Explain why the market needs this book and why you're the right person to write it. This paragraph is where you briefly share the personal experiences that led you to the material or describe your target reader. Authors often claim that their potential audiences are huge, imagining that universality is a selling point, but editors think in terms of market segments. Wild statements like "this book is for anyone who likes a good story" do not impress agents, but a thoughtful description of your target reader just might. If your book has a special market — it's ideal for book clubs or it's a great choice for YA fantasy readers mourning the demise of the Harry Potter series — mention this now.

Paragraph four: Now add your one-paragraph resume. Prior publications, contests you've won, MFA degrees, etc. Your tone should be matter-of-fact — bragging and false modesty are equally deadly. This is also the place to tell the agent what you're working on now.

Paragraph five: Thank him for his time and give him your complete contact information — phone, email, mailing address. Politely inform him if you are simultaneously submitting your book idea to other agents.

But What About...

Admittedly, none of this is quite as easy as it sounds.

There's always the question of how many agents you can query at once. Somewhere between four and eight is about right. You want to send enough out that you're not overly invested in any one agent's response, and a "no" is always softened if other possibilities are still alive. You can still open your email the next morning or walk to your mailbox with optimism. (Agents understand that most writers send multiple queries but you should still confirm this in your query letter, adding it to your sign-off in paragraph five.)

On the other hand, don't blanket the market with queries. If you keep getting rejected, you might need to rethink your query letter or sample pages or perhaps even the whole premise of your book. Once an agent has passed, they're rarely willing to look at the same idea again, so you don't want to query every agent in New York — which is another way of burning every bridge in New York — only to subsequently realize you've started your novel in the wrong place. Writers are often told to be blindly persistent — in other words, if you get a rejection you should immediately send out a new query that very day. But if you've been accumulating rejections for months, you may have to step back and re-evaluate your approach. And you want to do this before you've gone through your entire list of dream agents.

How long do you give them to respond? Most agents request six to eight weeks and then take more like six to eight months. If the initial six weeks have passed without response, feel free to send out another wave of queries. And be prepared for the fact that some agents never respond at all, not even with a form letter.

Rejection comes in several tiers. The worst is no answer at all. A step up from that is a form letter rejection. Then comes the form letter with a line or two scrawled across the bottom, even if it's merely "Thanks" or the even more promising "Try us again." A personally typed rejection is a type of praise, since it means you came close enough to the bulls-eye that the agent is willing to spend five minutes to tell you so. (Or it could be that you've been recommended to this agent by someone he values, so he's giving you the courtesy of a personal response.) The best rejections give suggestions for revision or urge you to try the agency again if you develop a new project in the future.

The level of rejection determines your next step. If you've tried several waves of queries and have received nothing but form rejections or silence, step back and reconsider your approach. You may have a weak query or a weak project. But if you've gotten some encouraging feedback, persist a little longer because it can indeed be a numbers game and the sixty-seventh attempt might be the lucky charm.

Try not to take the rejections personally. Everyone gets them. Everyone. A writer who can't handle rejection is like a surgeon who faints at the sight of blood or an airline pilot who is afraid of heights. Don't retaliate by sending off a bitchy reply, something along the lines of, "I'm sorry, but your rejection does not meet my needs at this time," and don't vent about it online. Or at least, if you must pour your heart out on Facebook or your blog, don't use the agent's name. Almost everyone in this business has Google Search set up to alert them when his or her name appears anywhere on the Internet. If you trash an agent in a public forum, he'll hear about it, and that bridge hasn't been merely burned — it's been firebombed. Plus, publishing is a smaller and more insular industry than you might guess when looking at it from the outside, so be aware that how you behave with one person might affect how you're perceived by another. Other agents might be reluctant to take on a writer who seems reactive and prone to wild outbursts.

Not to mention the fact that the agent who rejected you may have been doing you a favor.

Many agents reject good work if they don't have relationships with editors who buy that particular kind of material. As we've discussed before, agents work over and over with the same editors and specialize in a certain kind of book. If your project isn't a good fit for their list they may hesitate to take it on, no matter how well written — and this is actually a sign the agent is ethical and looking at the big picture. If an agent doesn't think he can sell your book, he's probably right, and the sting of a quick "No" may save you far greater disappointment down the road.

Sometimes if an agent offers a smidgeon of encouragement, writers might be tempted to say, "Is there someone else you could recommend who might be a good fit for this book?" In a way it seems logical, since agents know other agents, but asking one agent to refer you to another is generally considered bad form. One agent with whom I discussed this issue said she might see a manuscript recommended by another agent as "tainted." After all, agents are in competition with each other, so if this book is so great, why didn't the first agent keep it for himself?

There's one exception to the "never ask an agent to recommend another agent" rule. Obviously, you don't want to simultaneously send queries to two agents who work for the same agency. If it's a small agency, where decisions on whom to represent are made by committee, sending in multiple queries just means that committee will reject you twice. In a medium-sized agency, double querying is in essence pitting two partners against each other and this will not work out well for anyone, especially you. But in a big agency with tons of agents, it may be a different story. If a top-tier agent at a big agency sees potential in your book he may decline to work with you himself but be willing to introduce you to a less-established colleague. Young agents who are just starting out have more time to spend on new writers or on projects that lack blockbuster potential but still could sell.

Another common question: Should you offer an agent an exclusive, which means a period of time in which only they have the chance to read your book? If you've met an agent in person or through a recommendation, then yes, sure, give them an exclusive if they ask for it. There's also the chance that an agent who was blindly queried might ask for an exclusive, and this is usually a good sign since it means your query or sample chapters have struck a chord. An agent who asks for an exclusive is being self-protective. Every agent has a story about a time in which they took home a manuscript over the weekend, read it and fell in love, and then contacted the writer on Monday only to hear that he or she signed with another agent on Friday. So if they really like what they've seen so far, but they see in your query that you're submitting to multiple agents at once, they may ask for an exclusive.

But the exclusive should only be for a reasonable amount of time. Two weeks is standard. After that, you're free to look for representation elsewhere.

Send your queries out in waves and then, after six or eight weeks, send out more. Try not to harass the agents while your work is under consideration, even if you suspect they aren't reading it at all. An email after a few weeks to make sure they got it is fine, but if you start emailing every week, it won't help your cause.

Querying is a stamina game, but sometimes it does pay off. I recently met a novelist who found her agent in precisely the way that didn't work for me. She queried her way through the *Writer's Market*, although in this case she started with the Ss. Month after month passed, and she was almost back around to the Rs when she finally connected to the right person and, even then, another not-so-random factor helped seal the deal. This writer was studying at an MFA program where this agent was slated to appear on a panel, so the writer was able to say, "Since you're going to be in Baltimore next month anyway, can we have a cup of coffee together?" The writer is quick to admit that without that conveniently upcoming opportunity to meet face-to-face, the agent might not have paid any attention to the query. So it does happen, especially if you're able to use the query to set up a later meeting.

And what happens if two agents ask to represent you at once? Sometimes writers do indeed find themselves is this enviable position, and it almost always comes down to who they click with, and who they believe best understands their book.

If at all possible, hop the next plane to New York and try to meet them all face to face. You'll have plenty of things to discuss, including:

1. Does the agent think your book needs work? If so, what sort of revisions are needed and what is the time frame for doing them? Do his suggestions make sense to you?

2. What are your long-term goals as a writer and how can this agent help you get there? Step one is obviously to sell the first book, but the best writer-agent relationships revolve around similar long-term plans and dreams.

3. Do your communications styles mesh? There are agents who

do a lot of hand holding and others who will contact you only when there's something specific to discuss. It's like marriage. Some happy couples call each other from work every hour and others live on separate coasts, so there's no right or wrong answer. But you need to find an agent whose communication style is similar to your own, or one of you will feel neglected and the other will feel harassed.

4. Does the agency offer a contract? If so, what's in it? "The agent-client relationship used to be a handshake deal," one agent told me. "Even now, the main reason we offer a contract is to make the writer more comfortable." A contract will usually spell out what percentage of your earnings the agent will be paid (15% is standard for book and ebook sales, with 20% more common for subsidiary sales like foreign rights, movie deals, and the licensing of cuddly plush toys based on your characters.) Most contracts only cover the specific book the agent is representing, so if you're an established writer with many ongoing projects in different genres you may want to make sure the agent does not get a percentage of your pre-existing deals. For example, I have a longstanding deal with Fodor's to publish my travel guide, *Walt Disney World With Kids*. I brokered this deal on my own years before I met my agent, so he doesn't get any percentage of those monies, nor does he participate in my freelance magazine work, Internet publishing, or this particular book you hold in your hands, which I've published with a small press. I always tell my agent everything I'm doing as a courtesy, but he doesn't get involved with all the small daily deals of a freelance writer. If you've chosen the right person, this should be a non-issue, since no ethical agent expects to profit off work he didn't personally represent, but with so many modern writers working across so many genres it's worth mentioning.

Don't forget to ask the most important question: "Who do you plan to show my work to, and why?"

When you're having these early talks with an agent, whether you're choosing among two or three who are vying to represent you or simply vetting the one person who has shown interest, the most important thing is that you're taking the first steps in building a partnership. Writers may be so grateful that they become obsequious in these situations, but remember that the agent isn't doing you any favors. They make their living by selling your work, and without you, they can't pay their power bill. Your conversations should feel like a relationship between equals with mutual respect, common goals, and agreement, at least about the big things.

And the biggest thing of all is that you sense the agent's commitment to your book. The most powerful and famous agent in the world is no good to you unless she is passionate about your work.

Four Ways to Not Get an Agent

Agents want to know two things about you before they take you on as a client.

First, they want to know that you can write.

Second, they want to know you're not crazy. Just as some fledgling writers tend to think of agents as mean, some agents assume that writers are nuts, and let's face it, there's plenty of evidence to support that theory.

Just think back to your last conference or MFA workshop. Both the creative process and the giving and receiving of critique can be very emotional experiences, and writers tend to cut each other a lot of slack. When people are walking around wailing or cursing, we politely turn our heads. Not to mention that there's a tradition, duly noted in biographies and memoirs, of great writers whose personal lives were in shambles. Eccentricity is not only tolerated in this profession, but is sometimes viewed as evidence of talent.

Agents know this and are often fairly tolerant as well — or at least they are once you're one of their clients. But when they're first meeting you and are debating whether or not to take you on, your approach to them should be calm and poised, as if you're applying for a job. Because, in a way, that's exactly what you're doing, applying for the job of author.

Moving from writer to author requires a certain interior shift. You're turning from the world of art, which cheerfully accommodates wacky individuality, to the world of business, which does not. Agents need to see that you're capable of meeting deadlines, handling criticism and rejection, and working with a wide variety of people. An amazing number of would-be writers fail to realize this. When approaching an agent, they rant, rave, flirt, threaten, and do everything short of donning a t-shirt that reads "I intend to be a mondo pain in the ass."

So, task one is to have an excellent book that's polished and ready to show. Task two is to present yourself as someone with whom it would be a joy to work. Which means you shouldn't do any of the four following things.

Don't Brag

List any accomplishments such as publications, awards, and degrees in the fourth paragraph of your query, but list them simply, as if on a resume. Don't include praise from your classmates, your friends, or your mother. If someone whose name the agent might recognize, like a writer or teacher, is a fan of your work, it's better to ask this person to write a note on your behalf rather than to quote him or her in your query letter.

And while it's perfectly fine to reference other writers in your query, it's presumptuous and rude to imply that you're equal to or, heaven forbid, superior to them. You might say something like, "I loved Tom Perrotta's *Little Children* and have tried to bring some of that same suburban angst to my work," but avoid comparisons such as, "It's like *The Help*, only way better," or "I'm the next Jonathan Franzen." When you knock established writers, not only does it come off like sour grapes, but for all you know, the agent in question is friends with the person you're knocking. It's never smart to criticize members of a club you hope to join.

Don't Plead

Don't tell the agent that this is your last hope or that you're almost ready to give up writing altogether. Never, but never, whine about editors and agents who did you wrong. If your subject matter is autobiographical or sensitive — you're writing about the years you were homeless or being the daughter of an alcoholic — you should certainly allude to this, but briefly and calmly. Some letters from writers sound more like suicide notes than queries. Vent these dark feelings to your friends, but keep your professional correspondence professional.

Don't Stalk

Some writers think it's clever to approach agents in unconventional ways. They try to create something memorable, sort of like a "meet cute" in the movies, but to the agent, this almost always comes off as bizarre or even scary. One agent told me she was sitting on the toilet in the ladies room of a writer's conference when someone slid an entire manuscript under the stall.

If unchecked, persistence can also come across as stalking. Almost all agents have met writers who refused to take "no" for an answer and kept barraging them with emails and texts long after they had returned their manuscripts. Agents fear triggering an unstable writer, which is one reason they rarely provide feedback on manuscripts they reject.

Another agent describes a tale of doom that began with a huge bouquet of roses sent to her agency on a Monday morning with a note that read, "The query is coming." Flowers arrived every day that week, each bunch bigger and presumably more expensive than the last, and each note a little creepier, such as, "You'll have to wait," or "It's almost time." By the time the manuscript was delivered by messenger on Friday, she was convinced she was dealing with a certifiable lunatic and refused to accept it.

You're probably thinking that you'd never shove a manuscript under the stall of a bathroom or flood an agent with roses, but there are more subtle ways to cross the line. One MFA grad queried an agent who requested 25 pages of her manuscript. Her first chapter was 23 pages long so she quite rightly sent that. But as the days turned to weeks of waiting, she began to get a little crazed. The agent had requested 25 pages — was she wrong to have sent 23? Should she have sent the first two pages of the next chapter or run the first chapter off in a slightly larger font? Without consulting anyone on this and thus giving friends the chance to talk her off the ledge, she fired off a long and frantic email, asking if she should send additional pages, apologizing for being such a bad girl, and just basically rambling about how she was a beginner and didn't know what she was doing. It's easy to turn someone off by asking too many questions, sending and then re-sending slightly altered texts, or demanding constant reassurance. It gives the agent an unattractive preview of what it would be like to have you as a client.

Don't Be Unique to the Point of Weird

Being weird is not the same thing as being creative. In an effort to set themselves apart from the other thousand queries that came in that week, writers sometimes print their letters on lavender paper, use strange fonts, include drawings from their kids, write their queries in iambic pentameter, or create YouTube "auditions." Agents often see these stunts as proof that you don't believe your basic idea is strong enough to stand on its own.

I remember years ago, when my grandmother and I went to a wedding where the bride, in what I can only assume was an attempt to be whimsical, requested that the mashed potatoes in the buffet line be dyed the same bright teal color of the bridesmaid dresses. A big steaming bowl of blue mashed potatoes did not strike the celebrants as appetizing, and person after person passed them up. As we were driving home, my grandmother, who was a real stickler for tradition, kept going back to how the bride must have lost her mind to serve those mashed potatoes, and I finally said, "Well, she was just trying to be different, Boogie. Nobody's ever done anything like that before. " My grandmother looked me right in the eye and said, “Kim, if nobody’s ever done something before, there’s a good reason for that.”

Boogie has a point. Trying too hard to stand out with a gimmick usually results in the literary equivalent of blue mashed potatoes. Yeah, you’re different. But not in a good way.

Bottom line: Agents are looking for strong writing and they realize that the people who produce it often have more than their fair share of insecurities and quirks. But before they agree to work with us, they need to know that we can also be practical and charming and sane. Make sure your query letters and early conversations with an agent show the businesslike side of your personality and are aimed at building a mutually-respectful long-term partnership.

Chapter Six

Selling Your Book

Okay, you've got an agent. Now life is about to get really interesting. Your mind is probably teeming with questions, so let's look at them one at a time.

What are the steps in selling a book?

Your agent will approach acquisitions editors, who are just what they sound like, editors who work for a publishing house and whose job, among other things, is to acquire books for that house to publish. Some editors have the authority to purchase books without consulting other people within the publishing house, but most editors must discuss potential purchases with others, such as the publisher, members of the sales team, or other editors. The editor and the agent both act as liaisons between the writer and the publisher, but in negotiations the editor represents the publisher and the agent represents the writer.

Usually a book is purchased when an editor offers an advance against royalties. Advances vary widely, from a few hundred to over a million dollars, but the average advance for a debut novel in the present market is $5,000-50,000.

What does the term "advance against royalties" mean?

Advances are best understood through a case study. Let's say a publisher offers you a $20,000 advance, which is basically an up-front enticement for you to let him publish your book. To recap, the advance is usually paid in three installments: When you sign the contract, when the edits are complete enough that your editor deems the book "accepted," and the day the book goes on sale to the public. So that $20,000, less the 15% fee to your agent, will actually be paid to you in three smaller amounts that may be, depending on how long the publisher spends getting your book ready for market or decides to hold it in house, coming out over the course of one or two years.

The day the first book rolls off the press, you're in essence $20,000 in the hole to your publisher. After you've made up that advance by selling copies of the book, you'll begin to earn royalties on subsequent sales. Royalties mean that a percentage of each book sold — usually between 7-15% of the cover price — will be paid directly to you, the author. Royalties are paid twice a year, beginning six months after your publication date.

So let's say our mythic writer has a book priced at $20 with a 10% royalty. Two dollars for each book sold is credited to her, so she will need to sell 10,000 copies to have paid back her advance. After that, she will begin to receive royalties. Once her agent's 15% comes off the top, she'll clear $1.70 on each subsequent book sold. (This is an example, so we're using basic math for the sake of simplicity. In the real world other variables such as foreign rights sales against the advance and sliding scale payout may come into play.)

What happens if my book doesn't sell enough copies to pay back that $20,000?

That would mean that your book didn't "earn out its advance," and this scenario makes people grumpy — the publisher because they lost money on your book, the editor because they made the recommendation that resulted in their boss losing money, the agent because it's tougher to sell the second book of an author who didn't "earn out" on the first, and the writer because he'll probably feel like it's his fault, even if it isn't. But the good news is, you don't have to pay back the advance. As long as you fulfilled your part of the contract by delivering a completed book in publishable condition, the advance is yours to keep.

So I try to get the biggest advance that I can, right?

Basically, yes, but not just for the reasons you think. Obviously, you want a nice big check when you finally sell your book. If you're like most writers, you've gone into debt writing the damn thing over the last decade and need as big an advance as possible just to pay off your Visa bill. It's also an ego rush to get a big advance.

But the main reason you want a big advance is that it represents a big commitment on the part of your publisher, and is an indication of how much money they're prepared to pour into your book's publicity campaign in an effort to protect their original investment.

What constitutes a big commitment varies with the size of the house. A small house isn't going to have much money to pay for any book, even one they truly admire. So if a university press offers you a $5000 advance, it may be as high as they can go for anyone, and is certainly no reason to be insulted or worried. But if a big press like Random House offers you that same $5000, it's a sign that you're one of many first novels they've bought for that season and that they're basically laying small bets all over the roulette table, hoping that one of them pays off. A low advance from a small house is to be expected and indicates nothing about how committed your publisher is to your book. A low advance from a big house indicates your book is pretty much on its own.

So a big advance from a big house is the best thing that can happen, right?

Um, yeah, sort of, but once again there's a caveat.

Do you remember Helena from the writing colony, the girl I

talked about in the intro? She was the one who had trouble keeping down her lunch after receiving the big advance from the big house. Few people turn down money, but be aware that the big advance does carry with it a certain amount of pressure. A lot of people have bet heavily on your book. They'll put more effort into marketing it, and they will expect the author to make these investments pay off. Some writers handle this sort of pressure better than others.

Knowing they can offer bigger advances, will my agent automatically try to sell my book to a big house first?

Not always. Some books are simply a better fit for small houses. If your book is quieter and more literary, your agent may conclude it would do better with an independent publisher who can give it the time and attention it deserves and won't ignore you just because you're not a best seller.

Remember that books (and thus writers and agents) make money in two ways. The first is through their advances, and that's the way everyone tends to measure these things because the advance is a big showy splash of cash all at once. But the second, quieter way that books make money is over time and in the form of royalties. If a book catches on with book clubs or builds sales momentum through strong word of mouth, it's possible for even an author with a low advance to end up making a lot of money through royalties.

So, if your agent is afraid your book would be lost in a large house that's focused on their established best-selling authors, he may conclude that you'll do better in the long haul at a smaller house.

Why do I sometimes hear of first-time writers getting these huge advances? They don't have an audience yet, so isn't the publisher taking a big gamble?

You don't hear about it as much as you used to. In this market, even established writers aren't getting the advances of ten years ago. But every now and then a first book still draws a big advance, usually because the agent is able to draw multiple editors into an auction and a bidding war breaks out. Remember, the pricing of books is an extremely inexact science, especially for untried authors. If a book generates buzz and a lot of houses want it, things can get to the point that even editors who weren't invited to the auction jump into the mix. No one wants to let the next *Harry Potter* slip through their hands.

What about multi-book deals?

Several years ago, two-book deals for debut authors were fairly common, but in a tough economy, they've gone the way of the big advance. The advantage of a multi-book deal for the publisher is that if a writer's debut book takes off and sells well, the publishing house has locked up the second book for a relatively modest advance. The disadvantage of a multi-book deal for a publisher is that if the writer's first book tanks, the publishing house has still committed to publishing the second.

Writers tend to like multi-book deals because they not only mean multiple paychecks and the guarantee of more than one book in the marketplace, but they're also a sign the publisher believes in them. The disadvantage for the writer is that you're basically making a long-term commitment to an editor and publisher before you've worked with them. If it turns out to be a bad match and you're unhappy with how they produce and market the first book, you still have to honor the terms of the deal and give them the second. Also, by locking into an advance for multiple books at the outset of your career, you forfeit the chance to negotiate for a higher advance if the first book is successful.

Most writers will still happily accept a multi-book deal if one is offered, and most agents will encourage them to do so, at least if the offer is fair and the publishing house has a good reputation. And remember, even if you don't get a top-dollar advance, if the book sells well you'll eventually make it up in royalties.

If a publisher has a lot of editors, how does my agent know which one to approach?

It's a good question, because simply saying, "I'm going to offer your book to Random House," is a pretty meaningless statement. Random House has several imprints and dozens of editors.

If your agent has a personal relationship with one of the editors, naturally he'll start there. Or if an editor has a good track record of working with similar types of books or is known for having a preference for a certain genre, this could also make them a logical first choice. Or your agent might swing for the fences and try the most powerful editor within the house — someone with rank, seniority, or their own imprint, someone who can make a unilateral decision about which books to acquire and how much money to offer.

A power editor, like a power agent, comes with their own pluses and minuses. The pluses are that they have money to spend and the clout to spend it. They have egos out the yin-yang as well, so they don't like to let books fail once they've acquired them. If a power editor throws her support behind your book, you'll get a bigger publicity budget and more attention throughout every level of the house.

On the minus side, you may not have a warm, fuzzy relationship with a power editor. Just like a power agent, they get off on making the deal and then lose interest. Most power editors have so many books under their command at any point in time that they assign the actual editing to junior editors. Conceptually, this isn't so bad, since a bright and ambitious junior editor might give you better feedback than a jaded and distracted power editor. But if a power editor is so difficult to work with that he or she is constantly running off their staff, your book may be passed from person to person. One writer I know had a powerful editor bid on his second book, but that's the last time he had any real contact with her. He had six, count 'em six, editors work on his book over a three-year period, an experience he described as "nightmarish."

During the time a book is being offered, how much will your agent let you know about what's going on? That's entirely up to you and your agent. Some writers don't want to know each time an editor passes on his book, and most agents are more than happy to keep writers in the dark. Probably the most common agent-writer agreement is that the agent only calls the writer if he or she has an offer. But if you want more frequent updates about your agent's contact with editors, including editors who have said "No," you can certainly request them.

Remember, this period of time while you're waiting is a great time to begin work on another project. The *only* cure for the panic and paranoia that grips writers during this part of the process is to be working on something brand new.

What if everyone says no?

Some agents and writers hang in there together for years. Not every book sells easily and you sometimes hear of agents who were unable to sell a client's first book, but found a buyer for subsequent work. In other cases, if a book stays on the market for a long time with no takers, the agent and writer might choose to part ways.

What if everyone says yes?

If more than one editor is interested in buying your book, you have what my daddy used to call a "high-class problem." You may get the chance to talk to all of them and choose the one you feel is best suited for your book, or your agent may try to pit them against each other in an auction, in an effort to draw a larger advance.

If my book goes to auction, do I have to go with the highest bidder?

Not necessarily. When an agent announces an auction he also

sets the rules for the auction and can state that the final decision lies with the writer.

One lucky writer I know had talked by phone to all five of the editors who'd shown interest in her manuscript. She had a strong preference for one, but she and her agent still decided to take the book to auction. The end result is that the editor she preferred topped out at $150,000 and an editor whom she felt "really didn't seem to get the book" outbid her at $165,000. My friend and her agent discussed it and decided at that price differential, they should go with the editor she initially preferred and the $150,000 offer. The writer considered the auction a rip-roaring success, since she believes there's no way her preferred editor would have gone as high as $150,000 without the bidding pressure of the other four editors.

So yeah, there are occasions when a writer might choose to go with an underbidding editor if she feels that person and that house might be a better fit. Of course, if one editor offered $25,000 and another offered $100,000 your agent would have a stroke if you went with the underbidding editor, no matter how much you liked him. Nobody has that good of a personality.

Should I be worried or offended if my agent pitches my book to a smaller publishing house?

Not at all. The big houses tend to have more money to spend, but that doesn't automatically make them better. The highest offer isn't always the best deal.

On a recent panel at the big annual meeting of the AWP (The Association of Writers and Writing Programs), a group of agents discussed just this issue and pointed out that small presses, even if they can't offer advances, give a fledgling writer more time to develop a readership. If you've written a book with more literary than mainstream appeal, a small press may print 2000-3000 copies in its first printing. If they sell out, and the press goes back to print more, it's a huge accomplishment. Someone who sells 5000 copies at a small press is a star.

A large publisher simply wouldn't accept those numbers. Big houses have big overhead and a book needs to sell a lot of copies to just break even; one of the editors on the AWP panel claimed a large house wouldn't buy a book unless they felt they could sell 30-40,000 copies between hardback and paperback. That's a lot of copies. Most books fall short.

The biggest problem with a big house is that unless they perceive your book to have significant market potential, they won't take you on. Another problem is that big houses have big staffs, with a lot of churn and turnover at every level. Just as if you sign with a power agent, you may find your book being edited by a revolving door of editors. Even worse, the book may be "orphaned," meaning that the editor who acquired it either moves on to another position or leaves the house entirely. The orphaned book is then passed to a new editor, who may or may not be thrilled to have inherited a book acquired by her predecessor. This is a huge problem at the moment, with so many houses firing editors and so many books being subsequently orphaned. The woods are full of writers with sad tales of mean step-editors who didn't care at all about their little lost books.

This is not to say that all small presses are utopian places where everyone sits around eating granola and singing folk songs. In general, small presses have smaller staffs who aren't constantly in flux. They also are more likely to acquire books without best seller potential and to give their writers a better shot at getting established over time.

Besides the advance and how much I think the editor clicks with my book, what are some of the other factors that go into choosing the best deal?

Money and compatibility are the big issues, but after that there are several questions to consider.

1. How much are they prepared to commit to a publicity budget and how are they prepared to market the book?

2. Are they bidding on foreign rights as well as domestic? Some authors keep their foreign rights and have their own agents sell them while others grant foreign rights to their publishers. If your publisher wishes to acquire the foreign rights to your work, they should pay you a larger advance in compensation, assure you and your agent that they have a successful track record in handling foreign rights, and introduce you (either by phone, email, or in person) to the foreign rights team.

3. Do they plan to bring the book out in hardback or paperback? Although this perception is fading, hardbacks still do have a certain cache. There's the feeling, rightly or wrongly, that a hardback debut makes a book more likely to be reviewed in magazines and newspapers and easier for foreign rights agents to sell in the international market. Coming out in hardback also gives your book two shots at the bulls-eye, since publishers will put the hardback into the market first and then — usually anywhere from nine months to two years later — release the book in paperback. This means two chances to be reviewed, get into the stores, and find a readership. But, on the other hand, hardback is expensive both to produce and to buy, so many publishers are drifting away from it and releasing the majority of their books in trade paperback. (Trades are those oversized paperbacks that sell for about $14-$20, in lieu of hardback, which more often retails for about $24-40.) The lower price of a trade release may help your book find its readership earlier. A lot of people simply won't pay $30 for a book from a writer they've never heard of, and many book clubs won't touch a book in that price range.

4. The royalty payout percentage. Make sure you understand this, since it can play a vital role in whether or not, years from now when all the dust has settled, you've actually made real money on your book. Many publishers go with a sliding scale; for example, they might pay 10% on the first 5,000 copies sold, 12.5% on the next 5,000 and 15% on sales over 10,000. Your agent may be able to negotiate a better payout scale, build in bonuses if you hit a

certain sales figure, or even, in the cases of some literary novels, build in bonuses if you win certain prestigious awards.

5. Subsidiary rights and ebooks are another issue to consider. Most publishers insist on keeping ebook rights, since Kindles, Nooks, and other eReaders are an ever-growing segment of the market. Most of the time writers keep film and TV rights. If you've written a children's or fantasy book, or something else that could have merchandising spin-offs in the form of t-shirts, toys, or lunchboxes, this is a matter for negotiation.

If I don't have an agent, can I still sell a book?

Of course. While many of the big publishing houses won't look at unagented work, some do. Check the "author's guidelines" or "how to submit" sections of their webpages and follow them.

Be aware that submitting to a big house without an agent is the longest of all long shots. I was once at a writing colony with a young woman who worked as an editorial assistant for one of the large publishers and she said periodically the stacks of submissions would build up so high that they would have "pizza rejection" parties. The whole junior staff would stay after hours, order a bunch of pizzas, and spend the evening stuffing barely skimmed or totally unread manuscripts into envelopes. Ouch.

So if you don't have an agent, a more likely bet is to submit your work to smaller presses. You can also find these in *Writer's Marketplace* or simply go to a bookstore and check out who is publishing the sort of work you admire. Certain presses are known for certain genres and it won't take you long to discover who the players are in your particular field. *Romance Times* magazine is a good source of information on not just romances, but fantasy, paranormal, and mystery books as well. If your writing is more literary, subscribe to *Poets & Writers*, which has excellent listings in the back of each issue of who is seeking work. Many small and university presses run contests for poetry, short stories, and novels and publish the winners, and this can sometimes be the best way for an unagented writer to find a house.

In the smaller houses, there is no stigma for not having an agent. Since there's little or no money offered in most of the advances, the contracts tend to be a lot simpler. You can always have an attorney look at the contract if you have any concerns; look for a lawyer who has experience with publishing, copyrights, and intellectual property. You don't want to accidentally give away the farm.

And it's always a good idea to meet your editors in person if possible. First of all, this will be fun. You're being published and should celebrate that fact. Secondly, smaller houses really rely on the writer to help promote the book and a face-to-face meeting will allow you to thoroughly discuss the expectations on both sides of the table. It's also the start of building a long-term relationship with your editor and the entire staff, something that is far more likely with a small publisher than a big one. While big houses run on deals, small houses run on loyalty — among the staff and among their writers.

Chapter Seven

Contracts

The not-so-secret secret of successful contract negotiation is to know which points you might be able to influence and which points are locked-in and thus non-negotiable. You don't have to blindly accept any deal a publisher offers, but neither do you want to burn all your goodwill within the house by fighting battles you don't have a prayer of winning. Think of an author's right to complain like timeouts in a football game; you're only allotted a certain number, so you need to use them strategically.

This means you need to confer with your agent before the negotiations begin. He or she has probably worked with this house before or at the very least has seen plenty of industry contracts and should be able to give you a sense of where the negotiation points are. For example, the right to choose a book's cover and title almost always remains with the publisher, so save your breath. But your agent might be able to negotiate a more favorable payout percentage on your royalties. Likewise, a publisher almost always retains ebook rights and the author almost always retains film rights — but foreign rights could go either way. A quick chat with your agent should give you a sense of what you can realistically hope for.

Some issues that might be up for grabs include:

Ebook Royalty Rates

This issue is in incredible flux. Writers have reported getting anything from 8-50% royalty on an ebook. (We'll go into more detail on ebook pricing in Chapter 9.) That's a huge differential, since on an ebook priced at $10.00 this means an author payout of anywhere between $.80 and $5 per download. Multiply that by 10,000 ebook sales and you'll see why this can be an important line in a contract.

Why so much of a spread? Agents and writers argue that ebook payout should be significantly higher than the 10-15% payout range on a hardback, because ebooks cost the publisher nothing to print and distribute. There's very little chance they'll be returned and no chance that an overoptimistic print run could leave the publisher stuck with thousands of unsold copies, or "remainders." In short, since the publisher is assuming no production costs and no risk of remainders, it seems only fair he should cough up a greater percentage of the profits. Publishers in turn argue that the majority of their expenses aren't tied up in the production of the physical book, but rather in editing and publicity, and those costs are still there whether or not the book is published as a traditional book or an ebook.

Also consider that Amazon pays the publisher a 30-70% royalty, depending on how the ebook is priced. Ebooks priced between $2.99 and $9.99 earn a 70% royalty, so there is more money to share with the author, while ebooks priced under $2.99 or over $9.99 only earn the publisher a 30% royalty, so there's less to share.

Ebooks are growing as a market and lots of writers are on the warpath about this issue, so the standard royalty figures are subject to change over the next few years. You may have to take the percentage offered by your publisher, but perhaps you could have some protection in the form of a clause that says the percentage can be readjusted over time. You don't want to be locked into a 17% ebook payout eternally if the going rate changes to 35%.

Foreign Rights

Your publisher may retain the foreign rights themselves and this could work in your favor if they sell them aggressively. My publisher retained the foreign rights to my first book and in turn sold them to eight countries before the book had even come out in the US. The sum total of the monies they made through foreign rights almost offset the amount they had paid me as an advance, which meant that unlike most authors, my book was very nearly in the black before the first copy was shipped to a bookstore. Rounding the numbers for the sake of simplicity, it worked like this:

Advance: $65,000
Italian rights: $15,000
UK/ Australian/NZ rights: $15,000
German rights: $10,000
Dutch rights: $10,000
French rights: $7,000
Israeli rights: $2000
Turkish rights: $2000

So $61,000 of the $65,000 advance came back to the publisher through the foreign rights sales. That meant less pressure for me, that my royalty payments began earlier than typical, and that I have a wonderful shelf in my office where I proudly display my foreign editions.

But the reason this scenario worked out in my case is that the foreign rights department of my publishing house really got behind the book and pushed it. If, based on the house track record and prior conversations, either you or your agent don't feel your publisher would do a good job of selling your foreign rights, you should try to keep them. Then your agent (or the foreign rights team of his agency) will sell the rights on your behalf and any monies collected would bypass your publisher and come straight to you. (Less the agent's take, of course, and for foreign rights sales, the agent's percentage is usually 20%, not 15%.)

Foreign rights can also be a bartering chip to up your advance.

If your publisher offers you $30,000 up front for world rights, your agent can always either say, "We'll take the $30,000 but retain foreign rights," or "Yeah, you can have everything, but we'll need $40,000." Either way, it's a better deal for you.

Schedules and Deadlines

Production schedules and the deadlines embedded within them are set by the publisher and there may or may not be room for negotiation. Some publishers plan their seasonal catalogs years in advance and build them around a certain formula, i.e., "Every spring we bring out seven novels, nine nonfiction books, three YAs..."

In other words, your book isn't the only one they're focused on bringing out, but rather may be a single ingredient in a recipe that they don't want to alter. If this is the case, you'll have trouble persuading them to bump your deadlines back or to bring your book out any earlier than they'd planned. They aren't worried about your cash flow problems or the fact that you're pregnant or that your teaching schedule makes a May deadline tricky. They're worried about keeping intact whatever formula they've decided works for them.

Other houses, especially smaller ones who may do the majority of their marketing online, are more flexible. When my publisher and I were discussing the launch of this book, we basically pulled out our calendars and said, "When's good for you?"

Schedules can be an especially vital component if you're negotiating a multi-book contract where the deadlines may stretch out over years. You want to make sure the deadlines aren't too close and too overwhelming, but that the payments come at regular enough intervals that you can keep the electricity on while you're doing the work.

Bonuses and Escalators

As I mentioned earlier, some publishers will increase your payout rate when you hit a certain number of volumes sold and these "escalators" can really have an impact on how much money ends up in your pocket. For example, payout on a hardback might be 10% for the first 5000 copies, 12.5 percent up to 10,000 copies, and 15% after that. This is a way of acknowledging that once the publisher has recouped his initial investment, the writer deserves a larger part of the pie. Some agents are adept at working with these sliding scales so that the writer either gets to 15% earlier in the sales process or progresses to 20% as other sales milestones are reached.

Of course negotiating an escalator is easier if you know at what point your publisher considers your book a success. This can be a surprisingly hard thing to find out, since publishers rarely tell authors things like, "We'd be happy at 15,000 copies and thrilled with anything above that." Figures in and of themselves don't mean much: 10,000 copies might indicate a runaway best-seller at a small press, an average effort at a medium press, and a catastrophe at a large press.

You can ease around the issue by asking your editor the seemingly innocent question, "What's the biggest seller you've ever had?" or, if you're with Random House or another big publisher who's had stratospheric sales, "What's the best seller you've ever had in this division with a book similar to mine?" They may say 2000, 20,000 or two million copies, but either way you know what they consider a breakout hit, and this can help you and your agent figure out where to ask for escalators in the contract.

Another possible perk: Some publishers give writers bonuses, either in escalators or in cash payouts, if the book wins certain elite publishing prizes. It's sort of an extra "thank you" for bringing prestige to the house. Some high-end literary writers make more money in prizes and bonuses than they do in royalties.

Publicity and Marketing

If you see a pile of books beautifully displayed on a front table as you walk into your local Barnes & Noble, that doesn't mean the staff loves that particular author or even that anyone in the bookstore has read that particular book. What it means is that a publisher paid for that book to be displayed in that space.

Similarly, if you buy a novel on Amazon and the pictures of three or four other novels pop up with some variation of the claim, "If you liked that, you'll like this ..." a publisher may have paid for that too.

When a book is perceived as having best-seller potential, the publicity and marketing plans could become part of the contract. Cross-country book tours, premium space in chain stores, online banners, ads in magazines and newspapers — if you have enough clout as an author, you can demand the publisher spell all this out to the nth degree. But, frankly, if you're reading this book, you're probably not an established author yet, so it's unlikely any of these things will be offered up in a newbie's contract. Besides, no matter who you are...

Contracts Are Getting Less Specific

An editor at a major house, who was so nervous about the subject that she asked on three separate occasions not to be named, told me that the worse the economy, the fewer details are worked into a publishing contract. The terms of a contract, after all, are like a series of promises and no publisher wants to promise things they can't deliver. Publicity plans are being guaranteed less frequently, even for established authors, and publishers might also be reluctant to state precisely when a book is coming out or even if it will be published in hardback or paperback. Publishing is changing so fast no one wants to get stuck in a contract with outdated terms or language or one that commits them to spend money they may not have. This is especially true of multi-book contracts that stretch out over years. A friend of mine just signed a contract saying she'd deliver the last book of a three-book deal in 2016 and, as she said, "Heck, at that point, who knows if conventional books and bookstores will still exist?"

They will, of course, but given how many changes we've seen in the last four years it's natural that both she and her publisher would be nervous about a commitment that extends so far into the future. In light of the fact that no one knows what's getting ready to happen in publishing, you need to be especially aware of these two potential trouble points in your contract.

Right of First Refusal, or "First Option," on Your Next Book

On its own, this is a pretty standard request and no reason for alarm. Your publisher wants to make sure they don't take the time and effort to groom a writer and help her build her audience only to have the writer bail on them and go to a glitzier house once she's established. In most cases, what they're requesting is the right to take the first look at your next book, or at least your next book in the same genre. (If you write both thrillers and cookbooks, for example, you can't fulfill a right of first refusal by sending the publisher of your thrillers the manuscript of your great new book on barbecue.)

If you show them the manuscript of book two and they don't bid on it, you're free to take it elsewhere. If they bid too low, you're also free to take it elsewhere. It's smart to build in a limited period of time they can keep the book while they're making this decision — maybe 45 days. An open-ended right of first refusal can hold a writer up for months or years.

The important thing is not to agree to anything creepy, like a clause that entitles them to get a first look at anything you write for the rest of your life. One book at a time is enough. And watch out for non-compete clauses which would stop you from taking another book to a different publisher or e-publishing on your own. There's no need to be paranoid; most publishers have straightforward contracts that only deal with the work at hand and make reasonable requests. It's just that every now and then — usually with genre publishers, perhaps because many genre writers don't have agents and are thus easy marks — you hear of contracts that make outrageous demands. The sad part is, a lot of writers are so desperate to be published that they sign them anyway.

When Rights Revert Back to You

No one likes to talk about these things. Talking about when rights revert feels like bad karma, the equivalent of signing a prenup before a wedding. At the beginning of these ventures, everyone is so happy. So excited about this new project and all the ways you're going to make this the most successful book launch in the history of publishing. You love your editor, your agent, the publicity people, the foreign rights crew, the summer intern. They may have all just taken you to lunch and bought you a nice piece of salmon. So of course you don't want to think about what will happen if, perchance, the day comes when you all no longer like each other quite so much. The day when your book goes out of print or your publisher goes out of business.

But just as in marriages, not all partnerships end happily, so make sure an escape chute is in place. You don't necessarily have to talk about these matters while eating the nice piece of salmon, but at least discuss them privately with your agent. Most contracts have provisions that protect both sides in the event of a literary breakup or bankruptcy, and these standard provisions are usually sufficient, but you do need to verify that they're in there. Especially these days, when publishing houses are diminishing in size and power or folding altogether. You might not end up a publishing divorcee, but instead, even worse, a publishing widow.

Another point to consider: E-publishing has sparked a new wave of interest in the arena of books that have fallen out-of-print. When the rights to their out-of-print books revert back to them, some writers are putting these books on Amazon for Kindle downloads. Self-publishing an out-of-print book can provide cash flow for the writer and sometimes helps the book find new readers who missed it the first time around.

Many literary books have been trampled to death in the

stampede of big houses rushing toward best sellers. If their original publishers didn't appreciate them and allowed them to fall out-of-print, these books sometimes also enjoy a rebirth with a new, smaller press. Press 53, which published this book, partly built its reputation by re-issuing literary books that had been abandoned by their original publishers. For example, *The Land Breakers* by John Ehle was first published by Harper & Rowe in 1964 and rereleased by Press 53 in 2006, complete with a new blurb from the famously reclusive Harper Lee, someone Ehle has known for years. Lee's endorsement alone gave the book a huge publicity boost and a second lease on life.

So be sure to define when rights revert back to you. Is it at the end of a certain time frame? If the publisher declares bankruptcy? When the book goes out of print or sells fewer than 100 copies per year? In an era where POD technology has made it ridiculously easy for a publisher to keep a book technically in print — and thus under contract even if they aren't selling any copies — it's generally better for the writer if the contract specifies a date when rights revert back to him.

Remember, you don't have to hash all these uncomfortable points out in a face-to-face with your editor. Let your agent handle it.

But What if I Don't Have an Agent to Handle It?

As I said before, there are two major groups of writers who can successfully sell a book without agents — writers who publish with small or university presses and genre writers. These are two vastly different worlds and require different approaches to the contract issue.

Small Press Contracts

Because small and university presses rarely offer a significant advance, if any, agents are usually not tempted to get involved with these negotiations. The writer flies solo, which isn't as scary as it sounds, since small press contracts tend to be very simple. Most are boilerplate contracts, rarely more than a few pages long. Again, if you have concerns, have a lawyer look over the contract.

The two big bargaining points in small press contracts tend to be author payout and when rights revert back. An increasing number of small presses are avoiding one of the major risks that big publishers take. They may not send their books out into bookstores but opt instead to focus on online and face-to-face selling. Not shipping to bookstores means not having to hold money back for returns and — an increasing risk as of late — not being vulnerable if the bookstore goes out of business while owing the publisher money. Small presses also avoid one of the major expenses publishers have, like a big staff dedicated to promotion and publicity. Most often the editor and writer do it all.

Because small presses don't have these types of overhead expenses and market risks — and because they didn't provide a big advance — they often give the writer a greater percentage of the payout of a book. If a book is being primarily promoted by the writer and being primarily sold online or at readings, conferences, and workshops, the writer may pocket as much as 50% of the profits. The payout percentage should be spelled out in the contract. Note that small presses sometimes offer escalators too and they're likely to kick in much faster than at a big press; a book that sells 3000 copies may be such a hit that it lifts the writer to a higher payout scale.

A stickier wicket is the matter of how and when rights revert back. Remember Bill, the university press author I met at the artist colony and whom you met in the intro? As we discussed then, one of the advantages of a small press is that they keep books in print much longer than their big New York competitors. But this can be a disadvantage if your book wins prizes or garners sales that are beyond the scope a small press can manage.

Sometimes you hear of a book that begins life very modestly but somehow manages to zoom to national attention — for example,

Tinkers by Paul Harding, which was published by the three-year-old non-profit Bellevue Literary Press and then stunned everyone by winning the Pulitzer Prize. A small press is unlikely to have the distribution capacity and staff to handle such a boon. What to do then? I'd imagine that the idea of jumping to a larger press may feel icky to the writer. Sort of like dumping earnest Ernest, the boy next door, when the high school quarterback unexpectedly asks you to the prom.

It's easier to have a plan in place from the start. Granted, the *Tinkers* situation is extremely rare, but it wouldn't hurt to discuss with your small press editor what happens if the book sells beyond his or her capacity to keep up with distribution demands. Writers — or the newer larger presses courting them — have been known to buy their way out of contracts. Or small presses have been known to partner with larger presses when one of their books achieves unexpected success. You don't have to phrase this as "Can I dump you if I get lucky?" You can ask, "What happens if the book really takes off and we both see it could benefit from wider distribution?"

Genre Contracts

Contracts for genre books can look very different than contracts for mainstream novels. Payout might not be a percentage of the cover price but a flat rate, such as a dollar a book. Or the writer might not be paid based on royalties at all, but rather a one-time fee, such as $15,000 a book.

It all sounds very clear and up-front, but there can be pitfalls.

Publishers who specialize in certain genres, most notably romance, run an equivalent of the old Hollywood studio system where stars were signed and then put into pictures at the discretion of the studio, with the actors having little or no say about which films they were thrown into. Book contracts aren't quite that unfair and binding but can still have traps, such as contracts that state the writer delivers a certain number of books a year "written to the specifications of the house." In other words, they give you a formula and you follow it. If you're the kind of writer who can work like this and likes a steady paycheck, fine. Some writers find it dampens their spirits.

Genre publishers can also demand excessive degrees of loyalty from their writers. A friend who writes inspirational books once was approached by a publisher who demanded "an exclusive for life." I think that's a code term for professional suicide. Granting a publisher the right of first refusal for 60 days is one thing; promising a publisher you'll never work with anyone else your whole life long is lunacy.

Genre publishers tend to offer multi-book deals to writers they like. This can be good because it gives writers the assurance they'll keep being published, but it can be bad if the publisher tries to lock the writer into a low price point. One writer who does cozy mysteries signed a five book contract for $15,000 a book. The second in the series found a wide readership, a sales boom she did not participate in via royalties. And, even worse, she was contractually obligated to give them three more books at $15,000 per, even though she was now the imprint's top selling author.

If you're navigating the contract process without an agent, it's up to you to educate yourself. Websites like www.rightsandroyalties.com are a good place to start. Talk to other writers published by the same house. Once again, ethical publishers will happily connect you to their happy clients. Publishers with unhappy clients will hesitate to make these introductions, which tells you something right there. And if you feel real discomfort, get a lawyer — preferably one with publishing or intellectual property experience — to look at the contract.

The Psychology of Numbers

Excuse me for a minute while I drag out my soapbox and climb aboard.

Like publicity and networking, the subject of contracts makes a lot of writers very nervous. So nervous that they go into default mode. They're reluctant to ask questions about how they'll be paid or how their books will be marketed, partly because they're convinced the publishing world is incomprehensible, and partly because they believe agents and editors will resent their interference. The myth is that "real writers" don't care anything about business.

This is a very dangerous myth.

Publishing can indeed be hard to understand but that doesn't mean you shouldn't try. Years ago Mattel brought out a Barbie who, when you pulled her string, said, "Math class is hard." Feminists were outraged, claiming that the toy suggested girls weren't good with numbers, and the doll was taken off the market. Sometimes I think they should bring her back and rename her Writer Barbie, because a lot of writers also think it's cool to be bad at math. The truth is that payouts are structured around 10, 15, or 20%; if you're smart enough to leave a tip at a restaurant, you're smart enough to read a royalty statement.

Publishers no longer want writers who sign contracts — preferably with a quill pen — and then immediately return to their cabin in the woods to begin their second book. That's an old-fashioned view of what a writer does.

In the new world order, you, your publisher, agent, and editor are a team. No one expects you to understand everything about this world from the start, so it's fine to ask questions. This does NOT mean that you challenge everything they say or treat their council with suspicion. It just means that you show them you care how your book does in the marketplace and that you're willing to do what you can to help make it commercially successful.

Where did we get this idea that writers shouldn't care about business? To some degree it's been propagated by admired writers who have achieved high levels of fame. When these stars speak to groups or are interviewed, they may speak of the struggles of writing but rarely of the struggles of publishing. These famous writers are trying to give their listening public what they want. Readers are enchanted with the idea of books that seemingly sprang into existence intact, stories that were dictated to the author by the characters, prose that was perfect in the first draft. Writers don't like to burst this bubble for the same reason you don't want to take the audience behind the scenes of a play or show children at Disneyland how Mickey puts on his head. The illusion is part of what we're all selling, so the famous writers are perhaps justified in telling their listeners that the process by which books reach the public has a kind of magic.

The trouble comes when their fellow writers hear these stories and start to believe them too. If the writers you admire keep saying that they rely on their editors and agents to market their books while they focus exclusively on writing, it can seem that this is the right and natural order of things.

There's also the factor that many of these famous writers began their careers thirty or forty years ago, when publishing was very different. Writers went on tour. Serious literature invariably came out in hardback. The internet didn't exist. People had three-martini lunches. Publishing was a gentleman's game. And writers could indeed disappear for months or years at a time without being forgotten. In other words, our fantasies about publishing were born in an era that no longer exists.

Established writers — or masters like Tolstoy and Dickens — can be a wealth of information about the actual writing itself, because the actual writing never changes. But publishing has changed a lot. Anyone who broke into the industry even ten years ago launched their career in a very different environment than writers face today. So when established writers say they didn't worry about the publishing process, they are undoubtedly telling the truth. But their information is more of a history lesson than a practical guide to anyone seeking to publish her first book in the present marketplace.

Your editor and agent aren't looking for a recluse, a diva, or a dumb bunny. They're looking for a good team player. So educate yourself the best you can and don't hesitate to ask questions. It's all, quite literally, your business.

Chapter Eight

Working With Editors and Publicists

I tell this not-terribly-funny little joke in my workshops. Ready?

"They don't call the process by which writers get published 'submission' for nothing."

Like I said, it isn't that funny.

The moment your book is purchased, something that has been a primarily private activity abruptly becomes a team sport. All decisions from this point forward will be made in tandem with your editor and publisher. Writers often have trouble accepting this new reality, because they're coming into it straight from the creative process. It's hard to relinquish control over something that's been totally yours for so long, and almost invariably you won't agree with every decision that's made. But before you become defensive, you need to consider, a) there's a possibility they're right, and b) whether they're right or not, their opinion carries equal weight, and sometimes more weight, than yours. Some publishers are gentler about this process than others and some writers report that they were consulted about decisions along the way. But if you've signed a standard contract with a big publisher, prepare yourself for the fact that you may feel as if you've lost total control of the process.

Theoretically, when you sign a book contract, you're loaning your work to the publisher for a set amount of time — until the book goes out of print, the company goes out of business, or you reach a date far in the future. That's in theory. For all practical purposes, your publisher now owns your book. In fact, it's smart to start thinking of it as "the book" instead of "my book."

I know that sounds brutal, but stop for a moment to consider the language around the transaction that just happened, the transaction that made you so happy you probably celebrated with champagne. If you got an advance, you sold your book. "Sold" as in "you no longer own it." Books work pretty much like the sale of any other object. If you sell your house, you can't knock on the door six months later and say, "Why did you rip out my boxwoods and paint the door that hideous shade of purple?" It's their house now. When this fact begins to dawn on the writer — possibly because they're ripping out your back story and painting your cover a hideous shade of purple — it's a sobering moment.

Publishing a book is a long slow exercise in learning how to let go of something that not only means the earth and sky to you, but also something that, until very recently, existed exclusively inside your own head. This transitional period when the book is being edited gives you time to adjust to the fact it's now an entity unto itself. Not unlike a teenage child going off to college, it must begin to make its own way in the world without your total monitoring and protection. The first time your wishes are overruled in the editorial process won't feel good, but it's a chance to practice releasing control, a necessary skill if you hope to survive actual publication. A few months from now, you certainly won't be able to dictate how readers react to your work or what reviewers write about you, so you may as well start detaching now.

So when suggestions are made that you don't agree with, take a deep breath before you react.

For starters, as touched on above, there's an excellent chance that your editor or publisher may be right. You're a newbie and the other people on the team have been through this process before. Their suggestions are built on that past experience.

Secondly, it's important to remember that the author-publisher relationship is not meant to be antithetical. These people like your book or they never would have purchased it in the first place; they have a strong financial incentive to help it succeed in the market, so when an author develops a "me vs. them" mentality, she risks damaging all that good will. One editor told me new writers simply don't understand how much a pleasant attitude can help their cause. A publisher may put up with jerk behavior from a superstar whose books pay the bills, but you're not there yet, so being nice counts. If two absolutely unknown novelists are debuting books in the same season and one is a joy to work with while the other is a pain, who would you guess is going to get more attention from the staff?

And finally, if you want to maintain credibility with the professionals on your team, it's important to choose your battles carefully. Your opinion carries more weight in some categories than others; save your objections for matters such as rewrites, where you'll probably be listened to, instead of matters such as the cover, where you probably won't. If you argue over everything from the font of the lettering on the spine to the line they want to cut on the bottom of page 176, they will soon cease to listen to you at all. But if you're generally open to suggestions, they're more likely to take you seriously when you go to bat over the things that matter the most.

There are lots of decisions to be made as you build up to the magical day when your book goes on sale or your "pub date."

Rewrites

Writers have a variety of experiences to report about the rewriting process. Some editors have a light pencil, meaning that they make very few changes and consult the author before doing so. Others are much more aggressive, and if your agent knows an editor has a heavy hand, he may build a clause into your contact saying you get to approve any changes. Occasionally you hear of a situation where, such as in the story in the introduction of Helena and her big advance, an editor likes a story concept more than she likes the author's style. In these cases, she may excise the author's voice and add her own.

But, at least among the writers I've surveyed, that appears to be fairly rare. Most of them said the rewrites made the book better.

Most suggested changes seem to involve either the beginning of the story, or the end. Not surprising, since the early chapters are what must entice a reader to keep reading and the last chapter is the lingering impression that's left when the story's done. If a beginning doesn't work, the book won't be widely read. If the ending doesn't work, anything good that went before will be promptly forgotten. Either flaw can adversely impact reviews, word of mouth, and thus overall sales, so editors take a special interest in these parts of the book.

My friend Alison thinks her memoir about the death of her brother, *Name All the Animals*, was improved by her editor's suggestion that she add a final chapter that showed Alison and her brother playing as children, thus closing the book on a poignant but emotionally uplifting note. If you get suggestions about additions or changes and aren't completely sure they're a good idea, she offers this wise councel:

"Try it anyway. Everyone has a copy of the original, so there's no reason not to attempt the changes or additional scenes they've requested. One of three things will happen. Perhaps the changes will indeed make the book better. If so, great. Perhaps the changes won't work and everyone will see it's preferable to let the text stand in its original form. No harm, no foul, and you get credit for at least trying. It's the third possibility that most writers fear — that they won't like the revision and their editors will."

If the changes don't have a huge impact on the tone or theme of the book, a gracious concession may be in order. (Don't let your unpublished friends tell you this is "selling out." Knowing when to compromise is an essential skill in building a successful writing career.) But if the changes really make you uncomfortable, try to get your agent or other members of the editorial team drawn into the conversation. Rewrites are the decision that publishers consider most within the domain of the writer. They're more apt to listen to you here than anywhere else, so if you're truly unhappy, speak up.

The time and attention given — or not given — to your rewrites is a clue as to where you stand within the publishing house.

One novelist was thrilled to sign with a high-powered editor, thinking she was going to get the Cadillac of rewrites. But when she looked at the edited copy, she found many of the comments confusing. The editor kept inquiring about a character who had died early in the book. The author finally realized that the chapter with the death scene had somehow gone missing and sent it along to the editor, thinking they would start the revision process from scratch. But instead of reading the book a second time, the editor just told her to ignore any comments that related to the dead character.

"I thought editing would be a meticulous process," the writer told me. "So it was disappointing and surprising that this esteemed editor was only willing to read the book once."

Another novelist, who also signed with a well-known editor at a big house, didn't have any subsequent conversations with the woman at all. The book was purchased with great fanfare and then immediately turned over to a series of junior editors, all of whom stayed about six months, then left. "Just as I finished making the changes one of the editors would suggest, boom, she was gone and someone else was calling me to introduce themselves," the writer said. "And of course, each new editor wanted to prove she was smarter than her predecessor, so each one had a brand new set of suggestions. I changed the ending four different times before someone stayed at the house long enough to see the book through to publication."

Having an editor who loses chapters without realizing it or being subjected to a revolving door of rewrites is an unusually bad situation, but many writers experience a less-wrenching version of those stories, and they gradually begin to realize that their book isn't a particularly high priority within their publishing house. If you suspect you don't have your editor's full focus, that's because you don't.

Consider this. The fact you have a book coming out is probably the biggest thing in your life right now. If you have a phone session planned with your editor, it's the pivotal event of your day, if not your week or month. You sent in the revisions weeks ago and have been waiting nervously ever since, so anything the editor says during that call carries tremendous weight. She coughs. Does that mean she doesn't like something? She's unsure how to give you bad news? Or just that a sip of coffee went down wrong?

But this phone call that means so much to you is just one item on her to-do list for the day. Editors have always been overworked, and now, with financial cutbacks meaning that many are inheriting projects from their fallen comrades, they're under more time pressure than ever. They're dealing with lots of books and keeping innumerable plots and characters in their heads; if they seem to have forgotten previous conversations, or if some of their suggestions are contradictory, it's really not that surprising.

Instead of wailing that no one is paying you enough attention, make it easier for them to stay focused. It's a courtesy to periodically remind your editor of where things stand with your particular project. Several writers said that after every editorial phone call, they would type up a summary of what was discussed, then email it to their editor. This makes sure a record exists of the conversation if there's ever disagreement about what was decided upon, and also creates a sort of revision history in case you switch editors entirely.

Or you can touch base before the call to set the agenda. A very seasoned writer told me she always sends an email the day before each scheduled phone session, not only to confirm the time but to outline the points they'll be covering. "Conversations with editors are often rambling," she said. "It helps to decide in advance that, for example, we'll only be looking at Chapter 17 or discussing the character of the grandmother."

Don't be miffed or accusatory, but keep a pleasant tone, saying something like, "Hi, I'm just touching base to make sure I understand your comments," or "Wanted to confirm the changes to Chapter 4."

These summaries have the added benefit of helping you recap and focus on the key points discussed in the conversation. If your editor doesn't remember exactly what was said because he was busy and distracted, there's an equal chance you were so nervous that you went into a sort of trance. Listening too hard can lead to as many misunderstandings as listening too casually, so it never hurts to verify key points via email after the conversation is over.

Being creatures of extremes as we are, writers often believe they either have to make every change suggested or draw a line in the sand and refuse to make any. The reality is somewhere in the middle, but the essential thing is your attitude. They're trying to help you. So listen carefully, thank them for their input, and handle suggestions on a case-by-case basis.

Title

The title of a book is sometimes considered more of a marketing decision than an editorial one — which can be bad news, since publishers often defer to authors on editorial decisions but rarely on marketing ones.

They may use your original title. Or they may not, often because it's too close to a book already in the marketplace or it's just a really bad title. Publishers also know that certain words have universal appeal and might thus steer you toward titles that contain those words. The task of choosing a title is a bit like the conundrum of the query letter: you want to be different enough to stand out, but not so different that you're perceived as strange. Almost every editorial team I've ever seen has one person who's freakishly good at titles, so editors often defer to the team member who has a track record of choosing winners.

One strategy for compromise is that the writer submits a list of titles and the editorial staff chooses among them. That way the final decision is with them, but at least you know it's a title you can live with. Ultimately, you want readers to pick up your book and read it, not ignore it or run from it because the title turns them off before they even give it a chance.

Cover

Covers are a hot button for everyone and one of the things that cause writers to become very emotional. Crying, screaming, throwing up kinds of emotional.

This is unfortunate, because it's also one of the decisions in which we have virtually no input.

Well, perhaps I spoke too soon. Small presses often consult writers about covers, but in big houses this is a decision that falls largely under the domain of sales and marketing. Appealing to your editor isn't much help because he may be left out of the decision as well. There are tons of stories out there about books that got far down the production pipeline with a certain cover, only to have it abruptly changed — either because someone in the publisher's own sales department or a buyer for a major chain didn't like it. Agents and editors almost universally advise that a writer neither freak out over a cover he dislikes nor become slavishly attached to one he does; either way, it's subject to change.

Because so many writers react strongly to covers, editors usually don't show them to the writers until fairly late in the process. One novelist told me she saw her cover for the first time the day the UPS driver delivered twenty copies of the book — a standard gift to the writer just before pub date. She hated it, but it was too late to complain.

Even if you're shown the cover earlier, you may still hate it and it may still be too late to complain. Here's something to consider before you get too upset. Books are in the bookstores for about three months — at least unless they quickly catch on — so the majority of book sales have more to do with how an image looks online than how it looks if you're holding a copy in your hand. The miniature of a book cover that you see online at sites like Amazon is described as a "thumbnail." Covers with a lot of detail, especially photographic covers, may be beautiful to behold in print format but reduce to mush when thumbnail-sized. The movement toward online sales has prompted covers which have bright colors, easy-to-read wording, and larger, simpler images. Marketers want something that will pop in miniature, so they're more concerned with how your book will look on an Amazon website than on the bookshelves.

Bottom line? Don't fight this fight. You won't win and you might be wrong anyway.

Foreign Rights

Let's also look at foreign rights in more detail, because they're often sold at this point in the process, while the book is in production. The major international book fairs where foreign rights are brokered occur in Frankfurt in the fall and London in the spring. If your publisher obtained foreign rights and subsequently sells them, any monies accrued will go toward cancelling out your advance. If your agent retained foreign rights, he or she will work to sell them now and any monies, less the agent's percentage, will pass through to you. Either way, it's good news.

For this reason, it's wise to meet the people who handle foreign rights — either within your agent's office or your publishing house — and stress upon them your eagerness to participate in global markets. They often feel ghetto-ized and underappreciated, so a note of thanks when you've learned your book will be published in New Zealand or Korea is always in order.

Print Run

At some point the subject of the first print run will come up. It used to be that the print run was a huge indicator of what sales expectations were for a certain book. A healthy number was 25,000-

50,000 copies with best sellers having initial print runs in the six-figure range. A respectable print run for a literary novel, in contrast, was 10,000-15,000 copies.

But things have changed. With more and more small presses using print-on-demand technology, where they can print anywhere from one book to thousands with the flip of a switch, print runs are a moot point. And ebooks are seizing an ever-larger percentage of the market. Ergo, the size of the first print run is far less significant than it used to be. Many large publishers may open with 10,000 copies using traditional off-set-printing, while also setting the book up for POD, knowing they can quickly and easily print more books if sales takes off.

Besides, one of the most poorly kept secrets in publishing is that editors always lie about the print run, claiming it to be twice what it really is. So if they tell you the first print run is 20,000, figure it's really more like 10,000.

Print run may linger in the mind of the writer as a status thing, but, rather than treating it as a gauge of your publisher's commitment, look to the publicity budget instead.

Publicity Plans

Since, at least with books published by big presses, new books have a narrow three-month window in which to find their audience, publicity plans need to go into swing long before the book hits the stores.

In larger houses your book will be assigned to a designated publicist three to six months before your pub date. It's worth scheduling a face-to-face meeting with this person if you can, or at least having an extended phone call. Publicists and their assistants (collectively called your publicity team) can have a tremendous impact on your book's success and are just as important a part of the overall equation as your editor and agent. Treat them with respect, offer to help with the grunt work such as contacting blogs and newspapers, and keep them in the loop on anything you've planned yourself in your hometown. Most publicists maintain an overall calendar around each project so yours will need to know if you're not available on April 18 because you've planned a signing at the neighborhood bookstore or you're speaking to the local Friends of the Library.

In smaller houses, your editor may also serve as your publicist. The same rules apply, but you'll have to pick up more of the work yourself.

Either way, there's a limited time span in which you can expect to have the full attention of a publicist. You'll be in frequent contact for the three months prior to your pub date and then, in most cases, the publicist will move on to begin promoting the next season's books. Any requests you have after that — sending out books to the winners of blog contests, helping with a signing you set up yourself — will probably be handled by an assistant on the publicity team.

Blurbs

The first publicity task is to get blurbs, which are those little endorsements that published (and ideally famous) writers say about each other's books. Blurbs go on the cover, in the opening pages, in press kits, and on the writer's webpage.

Your editor will ask you if you know any writers who might be willing to blurb your book — this is another place where those contacts you've made at writing conferences and online can pay off. She will possibly browbeat other writers she's edited into contributing a blurb as well. Of course, there are a handful of very esteemed writers who everyone would love to claim as a guardian angel for their book, but a lot of these kind souls develop "blurb fatigue" through the years and begin to severely limit the number of books they endorse. So don't take it personally if you don't get a superstar to blurb you.

When you have a few people willing to blurb the book, they'll each receive an ARC (Advanced Readers Copy), which is a plainly bound and loosely edited version of the book. Needless to say, blurbs are intended to be positive — if a writer responds to the ARC with a proclamation of "Utter garbage," that statement won't make it to the cover.

Some people consider blurbs extremely important and link these sorts of celebrity endorsements to the likelihood of a debut author being widely reviewed. While no one would deny that kind words by Stephen King, Pat Conroy, or Margaret Atwood can help draw attention to your book, it isn't as if your book will automatically fail without them.

Your Website

If you haven't already established a website and blog, now's the time to do it. It's easy to get yourself up and going through sites like Blogspot or Wordpress, and your site doesn't necessarily have to be fancy. Some writers hire independent website designers and create very elaborate sites with music, rolling images, video, etc. That's great if you're willing to pay for it and sustain it, but a simpler site can work just as well.

The components you really need on your website are:

— An image of your book cover
— A picture of you
— A link to your blog
— An author bio
— A list of suggested reading group questions
— A link to your book trailer, if you have one
— A link to sites such as Amazon, bn.com, indiebound.com, etc. to make it easy to buy a copy once the book is out
— A page with some good reviews and blurbs, once the book is out
— A buy button so readers can purchase a signed copy directly from you (provided your contract allows for this)

Sometimes your publicity team will help you with this, but most of the writers I spoke with said they were on their own in terms of the website. If you decide you want a website designer, your publisher can direct you toward a good one, but you're likely to be the one paying for his fee. Some writers figure it out themselves, often with the help of their teenage kids/relatives/neighbors. But remember that a lame website often equals a lame book. You don't have to have a lot of bells and whistles, but a site that is clean, easy to navigate, and attractive speaks volumes about your professionalism as an author.

Trailers

Book trailers work a lot like movie trailers — they're two- or three-minute-long videos designed to entice readers to pick up the book. Just as with blogs, you can hire professionals to help you; some trailers are very sophisticated, almost like mini-films, and can cost in the thousands of dollars. Others are far simpler (and far cheaper) You Tube-esque affairs, primarily existing of a camera pointed toward the author while he or she talks about her book.

If a trailer goes viral, it can be a big boon to the book. And always, always, provide a link back to places where the viewer can buy the book.

The best way to figure out what you want is to look at a lot of trailers online, keeping in mind that, once again, the writer usually picks up the tab.

There are two schools of thought on how important it is for a writer to have a trailer. Many people swear they have no effect on sales at all, that they're done simply to indulge the writer's ego. Others believe that a well-done trailer can not only create buzz about the book, but that showing the writer onscreen is more likely to lead to them being invited to book fairs and conferences. (At least assuming they have a pleasant on-screen presence, that is. Many writers freak out when a camera is pointed at them, even if it's a friend's iPhone.) And some people are of the opinion that book trailers help sell a book's movie rights since they allow you to, albeit crudely, present the visual possibilities of your story.

No one knows how much trailers actually pay off, and they can be both time-consuming and expensive to make, so it pretty much comes down to whether or not you want one. I loved filming mine and since one of my writing group buddies is an independent film producer, I was able to get a cool-looking trailer done relatively cheap. For other writers, the very thought of going through all this seems overwhelming. Your call.

Reviews

ARCs are sent out to potential reviewers just as they are to potential blurbers, so if you have hopes of getting a review from your local paper, make sure your publicist has their contact information asap. But be prepared for the fact that few newspapers still do book reviews.

Publicists value some review sources more than others. If your book is reviewed in a major city paper, they will be dancing in the aisles; *People*, *O Magazine*, *USA Today*, and *Entertainment Weekly* also carry a lot of clout and will also bring on a jig or two. If there are magazines that you feel might be an especially good fit for your audience, discuss this with your publicist well in advance. My book, for example, was aimed at baby boomer women, so I was delighted to get a mention in *More*, a magazine that addresses the same demographic.

Four independent reviewers are major players and can have a huge impact on how your book is perceived.

Publisher's Weekly, perhaps because it comes out first (3-4 months before a book's pub date), is the most influential. A good review there, especially one that receives a star, is considered a very auspicious sign. *Kirkus* and *Booklist* are also highly valued; *Kirkus* is grumpy and pans a lot of books, so a positive review there is special cause for celebration. *Library Journal* is significant because they recommend books to libraries; with budget cutbacks, libraries aren't the major buyers they used to be, but it still never hurts to have librarians on your side.

If your early reviews from these sources are strong, your publisher may put a little more effort into your publicity campaign.

If your early reviews aren't great, you're not dead in the water, but you want to make sure that your word of mouth is strong enough to compensate. A recent survey showed that 87% of people trust peer reviews even more than they do professional reviews. This means putting more attention into reader reviews on sites like Amazon and, of course, the blogs.

Blogs

Blogs were huge for me. In the decline of newspaper reviews they have become one of the primary ways that authors find their reading audience.

A lot of blogs feature writers. Using your Facebook and Twitter community, you need to start zeroing in on which ones you click with, the ones who seem to have the same target audience as your book and those with a large enough following to make them worth your while.

Blogs not only put up reviews of books, but also author interviews and guest posts. Most bloggers are deluged with books from newbie writers and reviews are time-consuming, since the blogger has to read the book and then write the review. Author interviews require a lot less from the blogger, since all they have to do is provide the questions and you provide the answers. They love guest posts most of all, since you will basically write that day's post for them, on an agreed-upon subject.

Bloggers love to blog or they wouldn't have started these forums in the first place or worked to build up a large community of followers. But posting day after day can become a chore, so if you offer to write a post they're usually delighted. Many blogs are themed — I worked with one which was focused entirely on writing spaces and asked me to send them pictures of my desk via my iPhone — so it's easy to come up with the subject. Lacking that, they're usually interested in hearing how writers get their ideas, the writing process, other books that have inspired you, what it feels like to publish, or what you're working on next.

Giveaways sweeten the pot even more. On the day that your post runs, the blogger offers a free copy of your book to one reader. The most common giveaway format is that anyone who posts a comment in response to your blogpost is automatically entered and the blogger chooses one at random. Giveaways pull a lot more activity to the post.

Working with blogs is time-consuming, so you need to make sure you have the support of your publicity team. See if they will send out the ARCs to the bloggers in advance and, once the blogposts are up, if they'll also send copies of the book to any contest winners. This saves you not only time but money, since the costs of mailing out books adds up fast.

You want to schedule the posts to run just as your book is coming out. The public has a short memory, so it does little good to publicize your book three weeks before it's actually available for purchase.

In order to create a sort of crescendo effect, many publicists create what is called a "blog tour." Blog tours are infinitely less expensive than sending the writer out on an actual book tour where they fly or drive from one city to the next, and they're less stressful for the writer as well. Best of all, they're often more effective. Every writer has a horror story about the time they drove 300 miles to speak to two people; a blog with 100 + followers will actually reach more potential readers than you could ever hope to do sitting behind a table in a bookstore at some random mall.

In my case the blog tour worked like this. My publicist arranged for the book to be featured in ten blogs per day for ten days. The book came out on a Monday, so each working day for that week and the next I was on ten blogs. The form in which I was featured varied, but each post had my picture, a picture of the book cover, basic information about the book including quotes from reviews, and — by far the most important — a link that anyone reading the post could click and be directed to a bookseller's page.

This obviously drives impulse buys, since anyone who finds your post amusing or is intrigued by the subject of your book can buy it at that moment, while it's fresh on her mind. It's actually an improvement over a review in the Sunday paper, which requires the reader to either rip out the review or remember the author name and book title, then drive to the local bookstore.

Blogs helped my book get off to a good start in terms of sales and word of mouth. Even after the tour wrapped up, I would occasionally be featured on a blog and always noticed that day that my Amazon sales would climb.

Being featured on a blog is also a good networking boost. Along with the link to your Amazon page, you can provide a link to your own blog and thus introduce readers to your own site.

And… one blog leads to another. When you find blogs you like, snoop around the site. They almost invariably provide links to other blogs with similar tones and subject matter. The odds are you'll like those blogs as well. They can be a good source for your "son of blog tour" down the road.

My publicist provided the original list of 100 blogs that participated in my blog tour. I kept track of the traffic and it was immediately clear that some blogs attracted more readers, more comments, and thus presumably more sales than others. I winnowed these out and studied them more closely, clicking on any links they provided to other blogs. I cut her original list of 100 down to the 40 I found most effective and then, based on blogs those 40 were connected to and recommended, I began to build the list back up until I had about 70 blogs I felt were an excellent fit for my book. When the paperback for *Love in Mid Air* came out a year after the hardback, I approached that list of bloggers and this time the list was even more customized than the first.

Obviously, writing posts or doing interviews for as many as ten blogs a day takes a lot of stamina, so you need to start working on this long before your pub date. All the content came out over a two-week period, but I had been working on it for two months. I developed a list of subjects to blog about based on my vision of my target reader — we'll go into detail about this below — so that I could keep the posts individualized and fresh without having to think of a topic from scratch every time.

The posts and the visuals, such as the pictures of me and the book cover, were also sent in weeks in advance, so that on the day the posts went live all I had to do was check into the blogs periodically throughout the day, interacting with people who made comments. OK, I make it sound easy, but it's actually sort of a big deal. Checking in with ten blogs four or five times a day keeps you tethered to your computer, but it was only for a couple of weeks, and it my case it was time well spent. Getting that much feedback on my book that fast was pretty stunning, but also exciting. And interacting with potential readers is a large part of why the blogs work. If someone can ask you a question about your book, and you can answer it within minutes, you're building a dialogue with that person, and thus a relationship. They will likely feel more invested in you and your book and are more likely to buy it, read it, and mention it to others.

The blog tour had one other unexpected bonus for me. Blog reviewers often re-post their reviews on Amazon, Barnes & Noble (bn.com), and reader-centric sites like Goodreads. My reviews were generally positive, so my book began its commercial life with a nice clump of thoughtful, well-written 4- and 5-star reviews on all the major reader forums.

And if you're worried that a blog tour might have the opposite effect, relax. Some professional reviewers get off on skewering books, figuring that a bad review proves they have high standards and discerning taste. Bloggers tend to only feature books they like. So if they hate your book, odds are they will simply decline to feature you rather than put up a downer review. Individual people leaving comments will say all sorts of things, good and bad, but that's as it should be. You want lively dialogue around the book. Debate among potential readers is a good thing.

Other Publicity

Other forms of publicity such as book tours, speaking to book clubs, and launch parties also need to be planned in advance but take less time to pull together, so we'll look at them in Chapter Ten. Just be aware that if you are with a major New York publisher, that when your pub date finally comes, there will be a whirlwind of activity and your precious three month window to launch the book will fly by fast. Anything you can take care of now is one less thing you have to do then.

It's also a good idea to pitch ideas for feature articles about you, the writer with the new book and how you came to write it, to newspapers and magazines. Your publicity team will likely want to approach the big markets, like national magazines, but you should approach your local markets, such as your hometown newspaper or state magazine, yourself. These venues are always looking for stories, and a feature article is likely to sell more books than even the most stellar review.

There's one more task you need to get rolling on before your pub date, but it's more internal. Since it will inform much of your publicity push, let's look at it next.

Thinking about Your Target Reader

When you're selling a first novel, one of the questions that agents and editors often ask is, "Who do you see as your target reader?" This question is even more apt for the choices you'll be making throughout the publicity process; you can't hit the target unless you know where the target is.

Writers frequently respond to this question vaguely, something along the lines of, "Anyone who enjoys a good story," or "This theme is universal." They try to imply that their book has equal appeal for men and women, young and old, and cuts across all racial and national lines and thus has the potential to be a best seller.

Hmmm... yeah.

Industry professionals are rarely impressed by such claims. If they ask a specific question, they expect a specific answer. Give them generalities and you're just showing that you haven't thought about this *at all.*

So start thinking about it right now, for two reasons which sound unrelated but actually lead back to the same place. One: If your publicity team is going to pitch you to certain magazines or blogs, it will be because your book lines up with the demographics of those magazines and blogs. There are a million places to promote a book, so you need to spend your time courting the ones that will lead you to your target reader demographics. Two: Talking about the target reader is actually a gateway into a deeper type of question, the sort that interviewers, bloggers, and reviewers will be asking you repeatedly over the next few months. Start mulling these issues over now, so that you'll be articulate and interesting when the time comes to talk about your work.

Some authors write every sentence with a specific person in mind, almost as if the book is a letter, but if you don't write like that, you'll have to work a little harder to visualize your target reader. Probably the best way to zone in on the idea is to think back to what motivated you to write the book in the first place.

Let's say you have an 11-year-old niece and you've watched with alarm over the past year as she and her friends have become increasingly obsessed with their appearance, their clothes, and a disturbingly premature sort of sexuality. Perhaps, not completely by coincidence, your YA book features a plucky, tomboyish heroine and is in part a message to your niece that there's more to life than being popular and cool. So when an interviewer asks, "Who's your target reader?" you can say not just "10- to 12-year-old girls" but respond with the story of your niece and her friends.

Or maybe you're writing non-fiction and through the years you've become painfully aware that you and your weekend warrior athlete buddies are getting hurt more easily and staying hurt longer. This observation has resulted in *The Aging Jock*, an exercise and fitness book designed to help boomer athletes keep hitting the bike trails or ball court hard without sustaining so many injuries. So when the "Who's your reader?" question comes up, you can answer "50-year-old men," then follow up with the story of the sunny Sunday when a routine tackle took your buddy Dave out of the game for months.

Your target reader isn't just a demographic — they're also your motivation. This question is a great opportunity because it gives you the chance to explain not only why you wrote this book but also why, of all the authors in the world, you're precisely the right person to have written it. It's your chance to reveal your passion for the subject matter and the ways it resonates within you.

People want writers to tell them stories, both on and off the page, so get yours ready to roll. Describe the 11-year-old who's so desperate to be accepted by the mean girls at her school that she's on the verge of betraying her childhood best friend and losing her soul. Or maybe the 55-year-old man who hears the snap of his friend's ankle and for a nanosecond thinks, "Jesus, we're all getting old." When someone asks you who you're writing for, the best answers are always anecdotal. Readers may or may not relate to your niece growing up too fast or Dave hitting the gym floor, but it's a far better response than a big fake smile and a big fake answer like "Everyone!"

Like it or not, you're on the verge of becoming a public person. There's no way to publicize a book without giving strangers occasional glimpses inside your private world and sometimes feeling very vulnerable indeed. Start making decisions about how much you're prepared to show — and this likely includes explaining where your ideas come from and how they develop over time. You don't have to tell them everything and you don't have to dwell 24/7 in the public eye, but you do have to be real enough to be interesting. Being selectively self-revelatory now will not only generate more compelling blogposts and interviews, but it's good practice for what lies ahead.

Chapter Nine

Indie Authors:
The Brave New World of Self-Publishing

Traditional publishing doesn't work for everyone. Some writers can't get an agent, others find agents who can't sell their work, and some manage to make it into publication only to have their books go out of print. An increasing number of people have become exasperated by the whole casino-like system, and have decided to take matters into their own hands.

The good news is that self-publishing is now a viable part of the industry. It's less expensive and time-consuming than it used to be, and there are far more ways to reach potential readers. The advent of ebooks has been an additional boon, to the degree that some conventionally published writers are leaving their agents and editors to jump on the self-publishing bandwagon.

In this chapter, we're completely shifting gears, so it's worth pausing for a moment to clarify terms. Many writers, who feel that the phrase "self-published" carries a stigma, prefer "indie." So they are indeed indie authors, but shouldn't be confused with indie publishers, which are small privately owned presses who publish a variety of writers. Some people also use the terms "print on demand" and "vanity press" interchangeably, even though they are quite different. "Print on demand," or POD, is a process whereby books can be printed one at a time or by the hundreds, in order to incur minimal expense to the writer or publisher. Many publishers — big, small, and indie — use POD to both avoid crippling upfront payments and to ensure they aren't stuck with books they can't sell or to keep some mid-list titles in print. In contrast, "vanity presses" print large numbers of copies at a time, requiring large upfront payments from the author; you are, in essence, paying a company with their own imprint to publish your book, but selling it is entirely up to you. And finally, some indie authors offer only ebooks, some offer only print books, and some offer both formats. "Indie writer" refers to the fact that the author is self-publishing the work, not the format in which that work happens to be produced.

But no matter what terms you use to describe it, the important thing to note is that now, more than ever, some writers are making honest-to-God money by bringing out their own books.

Writers usually self-publish for one of the following reasons:

1. They feel rejected or spurned by the conventional publishing houses. They're tired of being kept out of the game by gatekeepers in the form of agents and editors.

2. They've had a bad experience — a dishonest, overbearing or inept agent/publisher or their books fell out of print.

3. They resent turning over so much money to the publishing industry and want to pocket a larger percentage of the profits from the sale of their books.

4. They resist relinquishing control over how their books are edited or marketed and want to have complete creative say over the finished product.

5. They have an entrepreneurial spirit and are comfortable with the idea of running their own business. Self-publishing takes you out of a "waiting to be discovered" mindset and allows you to discover yourself.

Ebooks are the most rapidly growing part of the self-publishing market, largely because it's so cheap and easy to make them available. Amazon, whose chief money-maker is the Kindle and who is thus deeply committed to promoting ebook sales, routinely releases glowing reports, but even the more objective *Publisher's Weekly* had this to say: "For the first two months of 2011, ebook sales were up 169.4%, to $164.1 million, equaling the sales of trade paperbacks for the two-month period." It wasn't really a shock when ebooks began outselling hardbacks, since hardbacks have been losing market share for years. But when ebooks start outselling trade paperbacks, that's news.

How long can the surge last? No one knows. Some people believe it will peak and the market will swing back toward conventional print. They point out that the first two months of 2011 may have seen those big jumps because so many people got Kindles or Nooks for Christmas and predict that when the novelty of these new gadgets wanes, so will the sales. Others argue that the surge in ebooks is tied to their price points — a huge issue we'll get to later — and suggest that if authors ever try to raise those prices, the sales bubble will burst.

But others argue just as passionately that we've barely scratched the surface of the ebook boom, and that there's still plenty of money to be made as the format expands. They believe brick-and-mortar bookstores will be nonexistent in five years and that print books themselves may someday be artifacts.

Who's right? No one can predict the future, and almost everyone who vigorously argues the point has a vested interest in one side of the argument. If you'd like to follow two fascinating ebook stories, check out these blogs. The first is called A Newbie's Guide to Publishing (www.jakonrath.blogspot.com) and is written by a man named Joe Konrath, who is bombastically pro-indie. Konrath refers to conventional houses as "legacy publishers," implying they're as quaint as hoop skirts, and a recent post directed toward writers seeking agents opened with the questions, "Are you dense? What the hell is wrong with you?" But if you can get past the slant and the rant, his blog raises some thought-provoking questions about indie publishing.

Another worthwhile stop on the cyberland tour is the well-written and surprisingly matter-of-fact blog of superstar Amanda Hocking, (www.amandahocking.blogspot.com), who made publishing news in 2011 both for her mega-selling paranormal romance indie series and her subsequent decision to launch a second line through conventional publishing. As you might expect, Hocking's take on the issues is more balanced than Konrath's. Since she described her meteoric rise as it was happening — 900,000 copies in her first year, netting her well over $1 million — her blog is an amazing study in how an unknown twenty-six-year-old genre writer from Minnesota became the toast of the publishing world.

Hocking is the first to acknowledge that she's a rare case. No matter which route they go, very few writers make a million dollars, so Hocking is no more a typical indie than Stephen King is a typical representation of a traditional writer. The real news is that quite a few non-superstar indies are making steady money. This is a friendly, open community, more than willing to debate issues and share their tips on what works and what doesn't — even to fess up on their actual sales figures and paychecks. Following the Kindle Boards (www.kindleboards.com) or articles on *The Writer's Guide to Epublishing* (www.thewritersguidetoepublishing.com) will give you plenty of food for thought.

I'm indebted to my friend Laura, who writes under the name LB Gschwandtner, for most of the information which follows in this chapter. Laura has released three indie books so far — her literary novel, *The Naked Gardner*, her young reader's novel, *Page Truly and the Journey to Nearandfar*, and she has co-written a humorous cross-genre novel, *Foxy's Tale*, with fellow indie Karen Cantwell. Collectively these three books are netting her a very nice monthly paycheck, and she plans to get more books uploaded as soon as she can. Laura has seen the indie rise from the moment it began, and has developed several theories on how a writer can grow a profitable business from her own desk.

How the Indie World Works

Once upon a time a writer who wanted to self-publish was forced to seek a vanity press, meaning that they were willing to pay up front for all publishing and printing costs. The price per book dropped as the print run rose, so the hapless author often was talked into ordering 1000 or perhaps even 5000 copies. He wrote a sizable check to the vanity publisher, assuming he would recoup his investment, plus profit, when he sold the books.

Shortly afterward, a UPS truck would drop off dozens of cartons of the books, which would be stacked in the writer's garage. They often stayed there until the end of time. If the writer wanted to sell the copies, he either had to haul them to literary festivals and hand-sell them one at a time or take them to bookstores and try to persuade the owner to put a few copies on the shelves. The bookstore owner typically said no, since selling self-published books is usually unprofitable. If he took a few copies out of the kindness of his heart, the writer then had to return to the bookstore at a set date in the future and either pick up the check for the one or two copies sold or, more likely, pick up the books.

Needless to say, this was not a system that worked well for the writer. Every once in a great while you heard of a book that found an audience through this improbable path, just as you sometimes hear of people winning the lottery. But most vanity authors never recouped their original investment.

As printing technology improved, a new system called print on demand (POD) emerged. Just as the name implies, POD allows the writer to either preorder a small number of books or have one printed each time someone orders a copy. There's much less up-front expense to the writer and no chance he'll wind up with a garage full of unsold books. There's also a new way to reach readers, i.e., the internet, so the writer isn't forced to drive around the countryside begging bookstore owners to stock his books. CreateSpace (www.createspace.com) is one of several popular POD providers, and since they're owned by Amazon and linked into their systems, that's an advantage in terms of online sales. A Google search will yield other available options, such as Lightning Source, Inc., the largest POD company in the world, which is owned by Ingram Book Company, the largest book distributor on the planet. Just make sure you're dealing with a POD system which has minimal upfront cost to you, and not a vanity publishing system, which requires you to buy a set number of copies up front.

Ebooks are even easier to produce than POD. Amazon will walk you through the steps of downloading your book and making it available to readers via Kindle, in a process Laura describes as "idiot proof." As of this writing, Amazon owns 85% of the ebook market, so some indie writers stop there. Nook, the device developed by Barnes & Noble, is preferred by some readers since its color format makes it more appealing for children's books, magazines, and nonfiction with pictures, but it remains a distant second in terms of market share and, at least for now, authors are less enchanted with its writer support. Smashwords is also popular largely because it is multi-format, allowing readers to download books to any device they choose, from Kindle to Nook to iPad and iPhone.

But no matter what format you choose, both the feedback and the money begin to flow quickly, at least by publishing standards. Amazon, B&N, and Smashwords all keep track of your number of downloads, display rankings which tell you how your ebooks are selling versus others in the market, and pay out royalties on a monthly basis. There's a two-month lag between when someone downloads your book and when the payment hits your account, but in the world of publishing that's a nanosecond. You can download a book in January and receive your first payment — either by check or direct deposit to your bank account — in March.

Exciting? Damn straight, especially when you recall that it took six months for that last agent to send you a form letter rejection.

But before you go to Amazon to start uploading your opus, make sure it's in the best shape possible. Laura suggests you work with both a general editor, to make sure the story is as strong as you can make it, and a copy editor, to proofread the manuscript for typos and lapses of grammar. (You can find both general editors and copy editors in *Poets & Writers*, by searching the web, by checking with your local writers' organizations, or by surveying your writing buddies. If you've followed my earlier advice and connected with a circle or writers, the odds are high that some of them can recommend editors they've worked with successfully in the past.) Writers may protest they want to get their books in the market as cheaply as possible, but Laura points out that 1) you can't simply throw anything out there and expect it to sell, and 2) these cash outlays are likely to be less than what it would cost you to go the traditional route. Agent searches, which often involve trips to New York or writing conferences, aren't cheap either.

When it comes to format, how wide should you throw the net? Laura says many authors start out with Kindle, then expand to make their books available via Nook and Smashwords as well. Some writers stop there and never enter the world of print at all, which, while certainly easy enough if you use POD, does require different formatting and a little more effort than an ebook. The chief reasons a writer might opt for print even if most of his sales are coming through ebooks are:

1. You can sell print books at book fairs, conferences, and other places where you meet readers face-to-face.

2. Even with the ebook boom, two-thirds of the reading public still doesn't have an ereader. Even if the ebook segment grows, it will probably never capture the entire market. Some people simply prefer conventional books and find a comfort and connection there that they can't quite reproduce with ebooks.

3. When it comes time to publicize the book, some reviewers insist on a hard copy — although this appears to be changing. (If a reviewer is willing to review an ebook, you can either gift them a download via Amazon or give them a coupon for Smashwords, which they can redeem in any format they choose.)

4. After all the effort you've put in and time you've spent, you might simply want the thrill of holding a copy of your book in your hands. Don't be too quick to pooh-pooh this as a legitimate reason. We work long and hard on our books and deserve these little moments of glory.

Price Points

When you're getting ready to launch your ebook, the single biggest decision you'll make is how to price it.

Remember how we said Amazon had 85% of the ebook market? This gives them a lot of influence and they're trying hard to encourage ebook authors to price their books between $2.99-9.99. The way they do this is offering a whopping 70% royalty payout to books within that price range. If you opt to price your book below $2.99 or above $ 9.99, your payout rate is sliced in half, to 35%.

Let's play with the math. If your ebook is priced at $2.99 with a 70% payout, you'll make approximately $2 each time someone downloads your book. That's significant money. If you had gone the conventional route, your publisher would probably have priced your ebook around $9.99. As we've previously discussed, publishers are all over the place in terms of ebook payout, but 25% is pretty typical, so in that case the author would receive $2.50 per download. The agent gets fifteen percent, dropping the author's take to about $2.13. This means you can charge $2.99 for your book and pocket almost exactly as much per download as a conventionally published author would get for a book priced at $9.99 — and it's much easier to sell a book at the lower pricepoint.

Despite this huge incentive to price ebooks for at least $2.99, many indie authors don't bite. They price their books at 99 cents. They believe that since they are a completely unknown commodity, they need to build a readership by enticing people to give them a try as cheaply as possible. And it's become a bit of a self-fulfilling prophecy. At 99 cents, an amount many people will spend without much thought, readers often download multiple books at a time without much regard to who the author might be.

Math time again. With a 35% royalty payout, a writer who has priced his ebook at 99 cents will pocket about 35 cents. At 35 cents per download, you need to move a lot of books to see a nice check at the end of the month, but this works for some indies, who say the volume of sales makes up for the fact they aren't getting much per sale.

Besides, this may not be the point. Indies who opt for the 99 cents price point argue that your goal for the first book shouldn't be to pay the mortgage or even the power bill — it should be to establish a readership. If your book is selling well, at least well enough to have a respectable overall Kindle ranking, Amazon will recommend it to other readers. This is potentially huge. So you want to price your book cheaply enough that a lot of people will download it and Amazon will begin to showcase your book... which hopefully leads to more downloads, an even higher sales ranking...and another turn of the publicity wheel.

Another advantage to ebooks is that you can play around with the price, changing it as often as you wish, with a mere 24- to 48-hour time lag. Some writers launch a book at 99 cents, announcing they'll raise it to $2.99 at the end of the first month. Or writers might have some of their books out at 99 cents, hoping that readers who try them and like them will buy their other books at a higher price point. Or a book can debut at $2.99 then go on sale for 99 cents if the higher price point doesn't work.

There's also a philosophical issue underlying this whole matter of price point. Writers, both traditional and indie, often argue that this flood of 99 cent ebooks is training people to expect cheap prices, nudging consumers into a mind-set that may be hard to break. They point out that the internet has already destroyed the newspaper and magazine business, by teaching consumers that information should be both readily available and free. And now we're on the same road with books, teaching consumers that they should be able to purchase four novels for the price of a latte or a gallon of gas.

There are a lot of discussions on the web about this, especially at the Kindle Boards, an independent message board unaffiliated with Amazon, where indie authors can share their experiences. Consider the various schools of thought before you price your book, and keep in mind that whatever you decide, you can always change it later and see if you make more money at a different price.

Covers

The cover of an ebook is just as important as the cover of a conventional book. Remember how we earlier said that all book covers are now chosen based on how they look in the internet "thumbprint" version? You want a cover that pops in the small format.

In terms of creating the cover, Photoshop allows you to play around with images and CreateSpace walks you through the process step-by-step. Laura cautions that "you don't want it to look amateurish," so you might opt to enlist the help of someone with graphic design experience. She also suggests you look at the covers of books that rank high on Amazon, especially indies, since those writers are clearly doing something right.

A quick scan of successful covers will show that most of them are relatively simple, with easily-readable font and bold colors. Authors with multiple books often design their covers similarly, hoping to entice a reader who liked one of the books to buy the others. (Amanda Hocking, whose covers show stormy skies in various colors, is a master at this.) Before you fall in love with an image, reduce it to thumbprint size and make sure that it translates well to the smaller format.

Reviews

There are two levels of indie reviews — professional reviews, which appear mostly on blogs, and reader reviews, those one-to-five star ratings that appear on the Amazon or bn.com sites.

In terms of finding professional reviewers, there's a growing list of bloggers willing to review indie work — as well as feature posts by indie authors. Ideally, you'd like the reviews to come out a couple of weeks after your book launches, so in order to accommodate the turnaround time, you'll need to get going a couple of months in advance. Use Google to assemble a list of blogs, contact the bloggers, develop any material they need from you, send advance copies, and make sure they have images of your cover and links to your book on Amazon, bn.com, and Smashwords.

Encourage everyone who buys your book, and indeed anyone you know, to post reader reviews on Amazon, bn.com, Goodreads, etc. If the reviewer is a friend, remind them not to report that they've known you since third grade, since this admission will immediately discredit their review.

The more reviews you get, the higher the odds become that some of them will be negative. This is inevitable, so don't take it too much to heart — unless they all comment on the same points, which may be a sign that your book has fatal flaws that need revision. An occasional one- or two-star review is a sign that real people are reading your book in significant numbers, nothing more. If you don't believe me, look at the review pages for Pulitzer-prize winners and best-sellers. They have plenty of bad reviews.

We'll discuss how to psychologically deal with negative reviews in the next chapter, but for now just be aware that the anonymity of the internet can make people cruel. Don't obsess too much about what Susie from Sacramento wrote, or you'll drive yourself nuts.

Ongoing Publicity

It's nice to have a big publicity push around the launch, but the true beauty of indie publishing is that you aren't under the kind of time pressure most writers face — "launch big or your book dies."

Indie publishing isn't a sprint, it's a long-distance run. When a book is published in the conventional way it has a two- or three-month window to establish itself in bookstores. If it doesn't — and most don't — the book is essentially dead. Indie marketing works just the opposite. There's often a slow build-up as a book accumulates readers, reviews, and begins to generate word-of-mouth. (Or, more aptly, word-of-post.) The most successful indie authors are those who rather allot a certain amount of time each day, week, or month to building their readership.

There are ways to directly publicize your work. For example, you can run a banner promoting your book on the indie-friendly site Frugal eReader for about $20, something that Laura has found almost always leads to a bump in sales. Enough of a bump to recoup the investment? Not always, but when it comes to promotion she says, "You have to look at it as a chance to raise the profile of the book. It's foolish to promote in several ways simultaneously, since you'll have no way of knowing which of the things you're doing is working. Indies aren't under any particular time pressure, so I'd suggest trying one promotion at a time to see which ones make a difference in your sales and rankings."

The overall sales rankings on Amazon show quite a few indie authors in the top 100 or top 1000 at any given time. There are also category rankings — you might be 920 in overall books but 87 in literary fiction, for example — and these can help draw attention to your work as well.

Because you can check your ranking and sales figures every day — or every hour — an indie author truly is running an ongoing experiment. Writers faced with sluggish sales or bad reviews have changed their books covers, titles, price points, and even the story line. And when a sharp-eyed reader caught a continuity mistake in one of Laura's books, *Foxy's Tale*— a character dropped her backpack off at home at the end of one chapter but still had it with her in the next — Laura was easily able to correct the text. "The flexibility of the format allows you to fine-tune until you have everything the way you want it," she says. "That's a luxury other writers don't have."

But this never-ending stream of feedback also has its dark side, with writers surfing Amazon for hours and becoming so obsessed with rankings, sales figures, and reviews that they're like an eleven-year-old with a new video game, oblivious to the rest of the world around them. Just as writers set a certain amount of time each day to publicize, it's equally important to limit the amount of time you spend staring at the computer screen. Blogs, Facebook, and Twitter can be worthwhile tools in the indie arsenal, but if you become too obsessed with upticks and downticks, you won't have time to write your next book. There's a sort of natural ocean churn to the rankings, with books constantly moving in and out of the top slots, so it's pointless to spend hours analyzing why you're up one day and down the next.

Likewise, the flexibility of the format can be a double-edged sword. Yes, correct your obvious mistakes, but know when to quit fiddling and let the book stand on its own.

Sample Chapters

At a panel on indie publishing at the 2011 AWP conference in Washington, D.C. the subject turned — as it always seems to — back to the issue of pricing. The audience was distressed by the idea that they might have to drop the prices on their books to 99 cents in order to compete with the other writers who had dropped their prices to 99 cents, and were bemoaning the literal devaluation of literature. The inevitable comparisons to a cup of coffee or a gallon of gas were bandied about the room.

One of the panelists made a good point. He said that a new author is an untried commodity and thus a tough sale even for a conventional publishing house — but with conventional publishing, the reader at least has the comfort of knowing this newbie was vetted by agents and editors before his work was tossed into the marketplace. Most indies are not only unknown to the reader, but also serve as their own agents and editors. In other words, the only person the reader knows for sure likes the book in question is the author himself.

The panelist reminded us that when a consumer plunks down money for a cup of coffee, he knows what that coffee is going to taste like. He knows that gallon of gas will make his car go. But buying the work of a first-time author is a true gamble. There are plenty of ebooks out there that are not only badly written by any standard, but riddled with misspellings and mistakes. Consumer skepticism is understandable, even at a low price point.

His suggestion was that authors follow the model of grocery stores that give away cheese samples. If they're offering a new cheese, they don't expect shoppers to pay $15 a pound for something they've never tasted — they give them a little slice. Writers can likewise post a sample chapter online and at the end say, "If you like what you've read so far, here's where you can buy the rest of the book." A link leads them to the sales page and under this model, if the reader is hooked on the story, he's more likely to pay $2.99 to finish the book.

It's a model worth considering. You aren't asking them to pay 99 cents on a total crapshoot, you're asking them to spend a bit more on something they already know they like. The sample chapter — presumably on your heavily-publicized blog — also allows readers to leave comments, which is a boon for writers. Indies should constantly look for ways to stay in contact with their readers. If you can accumulate email lists of people who have visited your blog or downloaded your last book, you have a great place to start with publicity when you get the next book up and available.

People Who Succeed as Indie Authors

This chapter opened with a list of reasons people go indie, but not all authors thrive on their own, just as not all thrive within the system. The most successful indie authors have these things in common:

1. They put multiple titles in the market, so that readers who like one book can quickly purchase another. (Genre books and series, such as mysteries, romances, thrillers, horror, and the paranormal do especially well in the indie market.) Before you

launch your first book, it's smart to have several others written or in the works. Some indie writers put out shorts — priced at 99 cents — which work a bit like the old-fashioned serialized novels Dickens used to publish in magazines. You get the reader hooked and keep them reading. Laura says, "The people who are making serious money publicize their work steadily and have enough different projects for sale that publicity for one book cross-pollinates to another."

2. They stay light on their feet. Indie sales are a moving target, and what works for one book might not work for another. Something that was successful six months ago, might not work now. This is a fiercely Darwinian world, so only the most adaptable authors will thrive.

3. They treat it like a business. The work has to be consistent, both the writing and the publicity. You have to enjoy, or at least be committed to, all parts of the process so if you're one of those writers who dreamed you'd just write the books and then hand them off to your editor, indie publishing is not for you. (But then again, you'll also struggle with the ever-increasing demands placed on writers in conventional publishing.) The most successful indies have a control-freak side to their personalities and enjoy handling all the components of their career.

They don't need outside verification to convince themselves that they're good writers with worthwhile things to say. Successful indie authors are more concerned with what happens than how it happens, and at some point in the process they've reached peace with their decision. This doesn't mean they'll never publish in the conventional manner, since many writers keep a foot in both worlds. It just means they've weighed the pluses and minuses of each method and make decisions about their careers on a book-by-book basis.

Chapter Ten

What to Expect Once Your Book is Out

Your pub date is finally here. Pop the champagne, because this is a significant watershed and also sort of a birthday. As of today, you're not just a writer, you're an author, and that, my friend — cue the Disney music — is a whole new world.

Writers are writers because they write. It's a verb-driven definition, focused on what the person actually does. Being an author is more about the role you play in the world. It's a public persona, a bit of a mask, and maintaining a healthy distance between the writer and the author will help you survive the next few months as you're reviewed, analyzed, praised, ridiculed, and ignored.

You don't need to develop a whole new personality, but there are many ways to create rituals that signal to your subconscious when you're transitioning from your real self to your authorial self. For some writers, pseudonyms clarify where their private lives begin and end. Or they have certain clothes that they only wear for readings; donning them is almost like assuming a costume for a play. I know one writer who listens to her "psych up" CD of favorite songs on her way to readings and another who only wears glasses when he's being "the author." When addressing groups, I almost always begin with the same story, and saying the familiar words is a type of self-hypnosis. It may sound silly, but writers are sensitive creatures and if we went out into the world as our natural selves, the criticism or presumptiveness of the people we meet would probably kill us. We need to develop ways — other than alcohol and drugs, that is — to slightly numb ourselves to the process. This doesn't mean you're fake. It's just means you allow some aspects of your life to be public, while carefully and deliberately keeping other parts private.

Launch Party

It's a great idea to have a launch party. Your publisher probably won't pay for it, but do it anyway. An independent bookstore in your hometown is a logical venue, since it makes it easy to sell copies of your book. That's how I did my launch; we served a wine named "Novello," got covered by the local paper, sold over 200 copies, and I was able to practice reading from my work in front of a sympathetic crowd.

Or consider thinking outside the box of the bookstore — the home of a friend, a restaurant, or the library can also work. "Friends of the Library" groups are often happy to host launch parties, especially if you're willing to donate a few copies of your book to the local branch or give a certain percentage of your sales to their organization. And one author I know launched at a $100-a-plate restaurant dinner where people received dinner, a signed copy of his book, and part of the proceeds went to charity.

Book Tours and Reading

For years, a book tour was the gold standard of author promotion. Publishers sent writers on the road for weeks, and the phrase "thirty city tour" was a sign of their commitment to the book in question.

But now the conventional book tour is pretty much dead. It's just too expensive to transport writers all around the country, especially fledgling writers who are unlikely to draw crowds outside their home towns. Readings aren't as popular as they once were, and it's humiliating to face rows of empty chairs. I'll never forget one particular bookstore where the owner had ordered fifty copies of my book and put an enormous spray of roses on the table. I sat there for three hours and sold one copy.

My friend Jeff left his wife and kids at home while he traveled for six weeks, using his own money and driving from bookstore to bookstore like Loretta Lynn looking for radio stations in *Coal Miner's Daughter.* Sometimes he had readings scheduled in advance and other times he would simply pop in unannounced and offer to sign copies. Jeff is unusually outgoing and perky for a writer, and even he confesses there were some dark days in his journey, times when he thought he'd rather kill himself than face one more Chili's or Hampton Inn alone. Another friend flew from New York to San Francisco — at least this time the trip was on her publisher's dime — to read to six people, four of whom worked for Barnes & Noble. My favorite story is of a writer who showed up at a bookstore in a mall to find an audience of three. He gamely began to read, only to have the cops burst in and arrest his entire audience for a robbery at the jewelry store next door. Seems the crooks had mistakenly believed a book signing would be a good place to blend into a crowd and hide.

Get the picture? Despite the fact some writers believe book tours to be the height of glamour and press their publishers to send them on the road, in reality these tours are hard on the ego and hard on the body. This doesn't mean you should never give a live reading, it just means you need to make sure it's worth your while. Book tours and readings work best when the authors do one or more of the following.

1. Go to a place where a crowd is already guaranteed, like a writer's conference or book fair.

2. Give the audience a little added value in the form of a workshop on writing. Many times, especially if you write literary fiction, your best readers are other writers. Lure them in with a free class and you'll probably sell books as well.

3. Only choose locales where you have an advance team. Showing up randomly in Omaha won't guarantee you a crowd, but if your best friend from college lives in Omaha, prod her into service. If she contacts the local paper, perhaps they'll do an article on you before your arrival. Or she can alert area book clubs and put flyers in coffee shops or on college campuses. At the very least she can drag in her own friends to fill the chairs.

4. Choose independent bookstores who do a good job of getting the word out to their loyal customers and will continue to hand-sell your book once you are gone. They often know of book club leaders who live in their area or send newsletters to their clients. If you offer up an article or author interview to put in the newsletter before you arrive, that can help pull a crowd.

To maximize your reading and signing experiences, interact as much as you can with the staff. Jeff says he didn't always sell a lot of books at the reading itself, but he thinks the fact the staff met him made them more likely to suggest his book to customers later. "You've got to look at a reading as helping you build word of mouth," he says. "Small independent bookstores still hand-sell to their clients, and if they know you, they're more likely to recommend your book."

Some basic rules: Practice reading certain sections, so you'll be smooth and relaxed. Don't be afraid to emote or to play around with the dialogue. It's okay to talk a little to set up your reading, but if a passage requires too much explanation, look for another one that better stands on its own. Consider reading two or three short passages rather than one long one.

The total reading should not exceed fifteen minutes; spend the rest of the time talking about your writing process or how you got the idea for the story. As one bookseller said: "If people only want to read the book, they'll just buy it. They come out for readings because they want to feel like they've gotten to know the writer."

Leave time for Q&A. Pretty soon you'll see that the same

questions tend to come up over and over, and your answers will become as polished as your readings. And be prepared for the fact that sometimes it takes a moment to get the Q&A going. Instead of saying, "Oh, well since there are no questions…" and bolting, allow a few seconds of silence while the audience gathers up their courage. If the group seems shy you can always interview yourself a bit, by starting it off with something like, "People sometimes ask me if the character Cassie is based on anyone specific…" Or, to lighten things up, you can even raise your own hand, and say, "Oh, I have a question."

If the crowd is not what you hoped for, it's important to stay gracious. Those two or three people did make the effort to come out and hear you, and the bookstore is still your host. A small crowd means that you might opt to make your presentation a little less formal, perhaps pulling chairs in a circle instead of you speaking from behind a podium, but you still owe the people who've come an enthusiastic and complete presentation.

Besides, sometimes it's hard to tell how successful a reading is at the time. A writer I know showed up at one reading to find three people in the audience, so he turned the event into a more casual conversation by stepping out from behind the podium, grabbing a chair and joining them. All three people bought his book, and the next morning one of them phoned his publisher and purchased fifty copies as Christmas gifts for her friends.

Bookstore Placement

Speaking of bookstores, you've undoubtedly noticed that some books have great placement, with stacks attractively arranged on tables just as people walk in — or better yet, in the window. This is rarely by accident. An established writer whom booksellers know has a strong audience might demand this placement on his own merit but in the case of a debut author, the positioning has most likely been paid for by his publisher.

So seeing 20 copies of a book on a New Arrivals table doesn't mean the staff loves it, or even that they've read it. It just means that the author's agent or editor did a good job of pushing the publisher to invest in bookstore promotion, something you might want to consider for book two. Especially if you search a bookstore for hours only to finally locate one battered copy of your book misfiled in the erotica section.

Of course, many bookstores have a shelf for staff recommendations and that space indeed is a reflection of what they like. And if you've shown up for a reading and been friendly, that ups the chances the staff will recommend you.

Book Clubs

Book club members buy a lot of books and if you can get in with established clubs it's a boon, since it usually means selling 8-12 copies in one swoop. Booksellers, especially independents, will often introduce you to clubs in their towns and some bookstores sponsor their own groups. Speaking to a local group often has a crescendo effect, since some members are probably also in other clubs; one woman in Charlotte invited me to four different groups.

If the book club is out of town, you can visit by Skype or do an online live chat. When doing a blog tour you can always mention your availability to virtually attend a book club meeting.

Two notes: Many clubs will only select a book in paperback, so if you debut in hardback, book clubs may be something to save for a second wave of publicity when the paperback is released. And if you find attending multiple clubs, either online or in person, too time consuming, you may not need to be there for the wine and social hour part of the meeting. Showing up for 30-40 minutes is usually enough.

Sustaining Buzz

In the first three months after publication, it's smart to focus on bookstore-related promotion, since this is the opportunity that will likely disappear first. But don't forget to keep your online campaign going as well. Create a Facebook page for your book and use it to announce new blog posts or appearances. Twitter a little more. Create an author page on Amazon and link it to your blog as well.

This is also the time that the blog tour you arranged prior to your pub date will begin running your posts or author interviews. On the day your book is to be featured on a certain website, be sure to check in several times to answer reader questions or interact with people who are posting. This can be great fun, and provide a nice lift to sales. Be sure to send a nice thank-you note to each blogger who featured you when the tour is over. These people are the unsung heroes of contemporary book promotion and deserve more recognition than they get.

Many bloggers are also happy to post their reviews of your book on Amazon, bn.com, Redroom, Goodreads, and other sites. Whenever I interacted with anyone who seemed to "get" *Love in Mid Air* or be intrigued by it — whether they liked it or not — I asked them if they would post an online review at the site of their choice. Most people were flattered by my request and happy to help.

You're probably thinking this all sounds like a colossal time commitment, and it is. For the first three months following your pub date, you're likely to be consumed with your publicity efforts, and it's easier if you just accept that. This is not the time to schedule a wedding, take a tour of Europe, or commit to lots of other writing deadlines. Your publisher will provide support, some far more than others, and it's essential to keep in regular contact with your publicist during this period to make sure none of the commitments you're making and she's making on your behalf fall through the cracks.

As we've discussed, social networking is not everyone's idea of fun but if you hate it, trust me, your resentment will show. It may help to think of the Internet as the modern equivalent of the town square, where you bump into people at the grocery or in line at the post office and have a little chat. Not all of those chats are profound and not all lead to deep friendships, but some are and some do. The Internet is your best chance to connect with readers — not just to announce when your second book is due or to alert them to a signing, although these are valid activities — but also to have conversations with people all over the globe who care about books. I've spoken to several writers who came reluctantly to the promotion arena and learned to love it.

Becoming Consumed

For some writers, Amazon rankings are like crack cocaine. You may find yourself checking them compulsively, every hour on the hour. Not good, since an obsession with sales is almost as dangerous for a writer as complete indifference.

You need to know how you're trending so you'll have some idea which publicity efforts are working and which aren't, but try to contain how frequently you log on and how fervently you analyze what people are saying.

Experienced writers find ways to manage the amount of energy and worry they spend on marketing. A speaker at the last AWP conference said, "Social media is only a waste of time if you waste time on it," so make sure your time is well spent. You might want to limit your online use to three thirty-minute periods a day — in the morning, around lunchtime, and again in the afternoon. One writer I know swears he does it all on the toilet.

Besides, over-promotion can backfire. Seasoned bloggers are quick to spot a phony, someone who pretends to be interested in literary discourse but is really just there to hawk her book. If you over tweet or mention your book title in every blog, you'll turn off potential readers.

Approach social networking as the chance to connect with people who have similar interests. It's important to mention other writers in your blog, to tweet when something good happens to someone else, to review other people's books. Don't join any group you're not genuinely interested in and don't talk about yourself all the time. Online conversations are still conversations. Ask questions. Respond to people's posts. You need to authentically care, and if you don't, social networking will indeed be a huge waste of time.

Online Criticism

One of the reasons the first months after publication are so traumatic is that you're hit with waves of feedback. During the writing process, you were only getting comments from your hand-selected circle of readers, and now complete strangers are sounding off on your book.

In the old days, when books rose or fell largely based on professional reviews in newspapers, a lot of power was in the hands of the few. If readers had strong opinions about your book, they might write letters to your publisher which may or may not have been passed along to you. But writing and posting a letter took some effort, so we can only presume that many readers didn't take the trouble, and, even if they did, there was a significant lag between the time the reader wrote his letter, mailed it to your publisher in New York, and it was in turn forwarded to you. And, most important, even if the critique was harsh, no one saw it but you, the writer.

Now feedback is swift and universal. A reader could hate the ending of a book, walk immediately over to his laptop, and broadcast his displeasure for the entire world to see within seconds. It's a democratization of the critique process, making all opinions equal and equally visible. Very few of us can ignore the impulse to read our on-line reviews, but keep a few things in mind:

It's worth repeating. The anonymity of the internet makes some people mean. They say things in a post they would never say to your face, and often they're just venting. Especially if the posters are themselves frustrated and unpublished writers. Many authors have traced back harsh reviews to find they came from people they know — I was once bashed badly from a former member of my writing group — and comments like, "How did this garbage get published?" often translates to, "Why was she chosen instead of me?"

Sometimes you get valid feedback that you can use to improve yourself as a writer and sometimes the reviews don't make any sense. An occasional negative critique means you're being read beyond your circle of family and friends and that your book is stirring genuine emotion in people, so don't freak out over every one-star review. But if a post is genuinely abusive, contact the site where it appeared. They'll take down reviews which have profanity or seem to have been written by someone who's unstable or has a personal beef with the author. Amazon is especially vigilant about protecting writers who are under unfair attack.

Here is something you may not have considered: positive reviews can be just as dangerous as negative ones. If you're overly praised for some aspect of your writing or your choice of subject matter, you may be tempted to repeat that in your next book…and the next. Authors who become too concerned with pleasing the public stunt their creative growth. Being aware of your strengths and what readers enjoy in your work is a good thing — just make sure you don't fall into a rut.

In the end, other people's opinions have exactly as much influence on your life as you allow them to. Some of the most famous and celebrated writers of all time have been brutally reviewed and current bestsellers are likely to have as many detractors as fans. While it's fine to learn from valid feedback, never, ever, ever let a review stop you from writing your next book. Consider the Arabic motto: The dogs bark but the caravan rolls on.

And… Nutcases

Every now and then you're going to run into a nutcase.

The most important thing to remember about nutcases is that their reactions have very little to do with what you've written.

Nutcases, almost by definition, show up with an agenda and thus their angry rants can be triggered by anything. Marybeth, who writes inspirational novels, once posted an utterly innocuous list of ten things to do with your kids over their Christmas break from school. One of them involved visiting Santa and so incensed a reader that the woman wrote a page-long diatribe about the reason for the season, opening with a huffy, "I can't believe you call yourself a Christian."

That very same week — holidays seems to bring the nutcases out in droves, sort of like carolers — I visited a book club where I too was beset. One member's opening salvo included the lines, "You disgust me. Not just your book, but you." She went on for some time, goaded by a couple of henchman who were practically chanting, "fight, fight, fight," while the other women sat with their faces frozen in horror. I glanced at my hostess, hoping she might moderate, but she was feigning an excessive interest in her dog, and as I realized no help was coming and the attack went on, the more I went into a type of shock. I was raised in a small southern town, so my default mode is docile and polite. None of my attempts to change the conversation to more neutral subjects worked, but at least I got out of there with my dignity and my jaw intact.

Does part of me wish I'd retaliated, giving her back the same anger and venom she showed me? Sure, and for the next week I kept reliving that morning in my head, dreaming up those sizzling comebacks you always think of once a situation is over. But when you're dealing with a nutcase, it's never smart to take the bait and argue back. The mud is their natural milieu, so if you descend there they'll have the home field advantage. If you instead take the high road — at least as much as possible, since writers are human and these attacks really hurt — you won't say anything you'll later regret, you'll avoid dragging in innocent bystanders, and the nutcases will eventually move on to new targets. Engaging with them only prolongs the drama.

When dealing with nutcases, keep these thoughts in mind:

1. First of all, congratulations. Nutcases are a sign you've arrived, because once you cross a certain sales threshold and have a certain number of readers, you're bound to encounter a nutcase or two. It's pure mathematical probability, the way every society seems to produce a set percentage of serial killers...or people who want to be writers.

2. Remember that not everyone who reacts emotionally to your work is a nutcase. The subject matter of some books may simply press hot buttons in readers. My novel is about infidelity and divorce, topics to which many people can relate, and events in their personal lives might color how they respond to the book. My friend Michael's thriller has controversial political undertones which, not surprisingly, tick off a lot of readers. Although his readings have sparked debates, he reports that most people keep their comments civil. It's really not hard to distinguish a person who's momentarily upset from a true nutcase. If you respond in a pleasant way — "I'm sorry my book wasn't your cup of tea. Who are some writers you enjoy?" — sane people will calm down fast. They may even end up apologizing for their initial outburst. But true nutcases just keep getting angrier, and they won't allow their victims to change the subject to more neutral issues.

3. Create strategies designed to keep nutcases at bay. On the week we were both blindsided, Marybeth and I met for bagels at the local Panera Bread. She explained that her book club strategy is to only visit for forty minutes. She lets them have their coffee klatch and social time, and then shows up for a brief Q&A. When she finishes, she leaves, saying that they'd probably feel freer to discuss the book without the author there. I think her plan is sheer genius. In turn I suggested if a response to a post gets out of hand, she disable the comments function of her writing blog. It's all about setting boundaries.

4. Practice go-to statements. If you speak to a lot of groups, you'll need to develop some reliable talking points anyway. Most

of the people who say weird things when they meet authors aren't true nutcases, just a little off the point. The more you mingle with readers, the more adept you'll become at gently steering the conversation back to relevant subjects. It may not satisfy them or answer their strange questions, but at least it keeps the experience from being a complete waste of time for the other people who have come to hear you speak.

5. Vent afterwards, but only to other writers. If you complain about this to non-writers they might suggest you retaliate — "Why didn't you kick her?" — because they don't understand how important it is for authors to maintain a gracious demeanor in public. Or perhaps they'll even think that on some level you deserve it — after all, you're famous now, right? And everybody knows famous people are fair game. Fellow writers are much more likely to get it and even to add to the list of clever come-backs you might have said. Pretty soon they'll have you laughing and that's always a good thing.

6. Look on the bright side. When I went online to announce that my novel had so much sex it drove a suburban book club woman stark raving mad, my Amazon rankings spiked for a week. People admire grace under pressure, and writers who can laugh at themselves. Michael became so adept at handling politically charged debates at his readings, that he was invited to speak at his state university.

7. Don't let them shake your confidence. Nutcases do not provide serious literary critique. They are a statistical anomaly and should be treated as such.

8. Most important of all: do not engage. Nutcases are like vicious dogs. You don't want to show fear in their presence but it's not smart to make eye contact either. This is just another chance to practice self-protection, and a chance to articulate your passion for your work, even under the most challenging of circumstances. How well you handle nutcases may be the ultimate test of your professionalism.

The Emotional Part

Everything involved with writing is a big psychological whirlwind, and, despite what you might have hoped, it doesn't get any easier once you're published. In fact, the three emotions below might hit you with special force precisely because they're so unexpected.

Envy

People are loathe to admit it, but envy is an inevitable part of the writing life. I've been on both sides of the envy seesaw, and it's no fun either way. Envy has always seemed to me such a sticky-feeling emotion, the kind of thing where you need to shower just after you admit to yourself that you're feeling it. No wonder we call it by so many other words.

Shakespeare felt professional envy, probably for Kit Marlowe — in fact, he wrote sonnets about it. Fitzgerald and Hemingway had a famously rivalrous friendship — as did Anne Sexton and Sylvia Plath. Melville got tired of playing second fiddle to Hawthorne...and Virginia Woolf, after reading glowing reviews of *The Four Quartets* by TS Eliot, went out to walk in the fields and tell herself "I am I, and must follow that furrow, not copy another."

So if you find yourself envying other writers, take comfort in the fact that you're in the very best of company. And then use the emotion as the writers listed above probably did, as an impetus to write. Tom Robbins called envy "literary Viagra," and it's the perfect stimulant to action. You can't let your friend get that far ahead of you, can you?

Another thing to remember: this is a street which goes both ways, and if you keep writing the day will come when you're on the receiving end of someone else's envy. They may envy you for a well-turned phrase in a writing workshop, or it might be an Academy Award for Best Screenplay. Whatever the reason, when you notice it you're going to feel, yeah, a little sticky. Because here's the interesting thing about envy. It feels no better to be envied than it does to envy other people.

When I sold my novel, another writer told me, "The publishing process will be full of surprises. And one of them is that your friends are not going to be particularly happy for you." Look at it this way: for years you and your friends have been lolling around in the same muddy pasture and there's something pleasant about a world where everyone is equally frustrated and unsuccessful. No one can get an agent, much less published, and you may have taken comfort in assuring each other such a thing isn't possible. Talking about publication seemed as fanciful as saying, "Someday one of us is going to fly."

But then it happens. Someone sells her book. And the reaction is not just envy, but surprise. Wait a minute. She sold her book? Actually sold it, and she has an agent and an editor and a title and a cover and all that sort of stuff? The land shifts beneath you all, and it's hard not to have a jumble of emotions, with envy certainly among them.

Now here's the conundrum. If your group is full of good writers and you're committed to helping each other, the news that someone's published is a boon for everyone. There's a little more of a crack in the gate, maybe your friend will ask his agent to look at your book. Maybe she'll help you when it's time to negotiate your own contract or publicize your own book.

But even if the stars align and you're able to help each other beautifully — and indeed it has happened among me and my writing friends — you still have to go through that narrow gate one at a time. Some people have to hang back and watch their friends precede them into the land of the published and that hurts. So the most important thing about envy is…

Accept it as a rite of passage. Evidence of how far you've come. Melville envied Hawthorne because he knew him. We don't envy people who are far above us or conveniently dead. We envy the people who are nearby, who seem just a step or two ahead of us in the process. The language of envy begins with, "It could have been me..."

So when your friends begin to improve in their writing, to publish, to win awards or be admitted into colonies, your envy is a sign that you're not that far behind them. Painful as it is, you've moved a step closer to publication.

Because if it could have been you, someday it will be.

Doubt

There's a great myth that once writers have sold a book, they've taken the first steps on a well-mapped path to a long and fruitful career. The reality is that it takes a long time for a book to come out, longer still for the marketplace to declare whether or not it's a success, and thus first-time writers exist — sometimes for years — in limbo. Some writers debut with multi-book contracts and have a strong sense of what their next move should be, i.e., writing the books to fulfill those contracts. But for most of us, uncertainty is built into the process.

The doubt is compounded by the fact that our agents and editors rarely pay us as much attention as we thought they would. Their own careers are designed so that their focus is on the project at hand, which means that there will be long periods wherein you and your book languish unattended. A busy editor, distracted agent, and anxious writer often adds up to plenty of misunderstandings as it seems that their attention comes in waves that recede just when you need it most.

Recently a woman I know signed with an agent and we all took her to dinner to celebrate. The other published writer in the group and I — our friends call us "the lucky ones" — decided we should bring flowers too. She deserved for us to make a big deal about it, we agreed as we were waiting for the roses to be wrapped, and then we looked at each other and said in perfect unison, "because this is the last happy day she'll ever have."

Now that's rather dark. We were being rather sarcastic. Neither of us would opt to turn back the hands of time to the days before we published. But the truth is that writers enter the publication process as innocents and emerge as grizzled war veterans. You never recapture that first blush of optimism and — even if you have periods of success, even if you are indeed one of the lucky ones — publishing is full of compromises and setbacks.

It never feels the way you thought it would feel.

Moments of success — you finish a draft, get an agent, sell your book, or reach your pub date — are often followed by post-partum crashes. I spoke to many writers who described how, just as they reached the point where they thought they would be the most gratified, they slid into depression and ennui.

At these times, all you can really do is practice extreme emotional self-care. Get plenty of sleep, eat well, avoid the crazymakers in your life, and plan little comfort rituals such as massages, movies, homemade bread, a weekend at the beach or whatever works for you. And embrace the universal truth that a big push is often followed by a fallow period, in which you feel as if all you can do is sit there and wait for news. Some writers step back from things at this point and others feel better if they start a new project — we'll talk more about this in the next chapter — but whatever you do, go easy on yourself. You're not going crazy. It just feels that way.

Disappointment

Okay, so finishing the first draft, finding an agent, publishing the book, delivering the commencement address at your old school, and (I'd imagine) winning the Pulitzer, we know that none of these things change your life as much as you think they will. What we don't know is how much this is going to disappoint us.

Most writers are unaware of the fantasies they have about publication. In fact, I suspect that if you did a survey, most writers would claim they are realists, with few fantasies at all. And yet we must have them, for most of us are utterly gobsmacked by the profound sense of disappointment that follows when we reach the long-awaited goal and aren't rewarded with the long-awaited feelings.

Several factors are at work here. One is that we're schooled to compare ourselves to only the most successful of authors and forget that when a breakout book like *The Help* is lauded from every corner it's precisely because it's such an anomaly. News becomes news when a story is unusual, so remarkable successes get all the press and the far-more-typical story of modest or partial success is never reported. Thus writers who are having an average or even above-average experience feel like failures, because they're comparing themselves to an author whose trajectory was exceptionally rare.

Another factor: no degree of success will shield you from every negative experience. There will still be bad reviews, readings where nobody shows, the fact that the book has been out for six months and your older brother keeps reminding you he hasn't found time to read it. And nothing, even the most fabulous level of sales, can spare you from the fact you now have to do it all over again. There are many stories of writers who soar with their first books only to falter with their second. The blank page is the great equalizer, and writers who feel that publishing one book somehow makes it easier to write the next often suffer the most profound disappointments of all.

And, finally, the series of compromises that the process requires eventually take their own kind of emotional toll. My friend Ed is a short story writer who is having a breakthrough year, with his work published in a variety of anthologies. Yet he showed up at our last writer group meeting completely morose, because one of his stories had been edited beyond recognition and another was published without the promised artwork, which was a major clue to the wit of the story. When things happen, they often don't happen as you expected them to — and naturally you're disappointed. Of course you want the reality of publication to live up to the image you had in your mind.

But just as being a writer is a complex task, so is being an author, and success rarely arrives unalloyed. You've got to find ways to be happy in the process. It will never be what you thought. Reviews will be unfair, sales will ebb and flow, people will go back on their word, and any success you achieve will be slippery and tenuous. There may even be times when you don't quite recognize the words before you as your own. But if you say to yourself, "I can only be happy if things turn out *exactly* as I envisioned them," you're basically deciding to never be happy.

It helps to focus on the people who have read and enjoyed your book. I cherish an online review by an anonymous reader who wrote a single sentence: "While I was reading this book I didn't feel so alone." And I remember one time when a little goth dark-eyed waitress in a sushi restaurant saw me with my laptop and asked if I was a writer. When I said yes, she said, "Reading sustains me," and in that moment her whole face lit up and she became suddenly porous with joy.

Publishing is one long exercise in learning to get over yourself. And in those times of envy, doubt, and disappointment, all you can do is step back and remember why you were drawn to writing in the first place. It's truly one of the last noble quests people can go on, a type of internal crusade. We've all read books that sustained us, and if you write something that, even momentarily, sustains someone else, that has to be good enough.

Chapter Eleven

The Fifth of July

If you're like most writers, you'll experience a sharp drop off in activity about three months after your pub date. Whether it was seventy-six trombones or your sister with a kazoo, the morning will come when you wake up and realize your personal parade has pretty much passed.

Your first question may be, "Was the launch successful?" but you'll have to wait for the answer. Because booksellers have 90 days to send the books back to the publisher, during the first few months after your pub date, your editor won't tell you anything about how your book is doing. The reason is they don't know. They know how many have been shipped to booksellers but not how many they'll get back and thus they can't predict when, or if, the writer will go into the black and start earning royalties. The dreaded phrase "returns were higher than anticipated" has caused many a first-time novelist to jump off the proverbial bridge. Or perhaps the literal bridge.

This final cycle of waiting can be the back-breaking straw for the writer. It's normal to feel bad because one avenue for selling your book and reaching your public is beginning to shut down for you. But instead of thinking "it's over," turn your attention to avenues that remain open. Some independent bookstores keep books in stock longer and thus give the writer more of a chance to establish word of mouth. And of course books remain for sale on the Internet long after they've been pulled from the big chain bookstores, so this is the time to redouble your online publicity efforts. It's not uncommon for a book to come and go relatively unnoticed in the stores but develop a second life gradually, through online sales.

Sometimes this echo life of a book has more potential than the initial marketing shove, and it's far more humane than the first three months when you constantly hear a clock ticking in your head. Bookstore sales may be a sprint, but online sales allow you to build an audience slowly, reach out to book clubs, find a fan base. So spend this time devoting maybe 30 additional minutes a day to online networking.

And keep your chin up. First novels don't have to sell a million copies to make an impact. It's nice if they do — everyone wants to be a breakout hit — but books that sell modestly but consistently can keep authors relevant to their publishers. Which is absolutely necessary if you want to sell book two and book three.

What You're Writing Next

You've probably already returned to writing something new but if you haven't, it's essential that after the first three months passes, you begin to wean yourself off the adrenaline rush of launching the first book and turn your attention to a new project. It doesn't have to be a big project. (If you want to start book two immediately, bully for you. I'm just saying you don't have to.) Perhaps you should explore another genre; after a bout of fiction, I always find myself hungry for the research and interaction of non-fiction and after a bout of non-fiction I begin to miss the creative freedom of fiction. If you were burned out by the effort it took to produce a book-length work, switch to short stories, poetry, essays, magazine articles. It's more important to start writing again than it is to worry about what you write.

Cross-genre work is not only a psychological relief, but can also help you build a career. Every single one of the full-time writers I know have two very specific things in common: they always have more than one project going at a time and they all write across multiple genres. Very, very few people in this industry can survive being a one-trick pony, so it's not only a nice mental break to segue into a fresh genre, it's a savvy strategic move as well.

Grants

Post-publication is also a good time to apply for grants. Some, like the Guggenheim, McArthur, and NEA, not only are the ultimate in status but give you serious money, so every writer on the planet is after them. Apply, but consider them a long shot.

Other grants are smaller, more localized, and less competitive. Most states award arts grants, and some cities do as well, and there are any number of independent foundations that provide funding for writers. You can research these online or through *Poets & Writers* magazine.

Prizes

It's a tremendous boon if your book wins a prize. Once again, you can research possibilities online or through *Poets & Writers.* There are prizes that you don't apply for — and these are snootily indicated with the single line "There is no application process." Other prizes do require that you submit copies of your book. Your editor or publicity team are likely happy to help you with this, even if they've essentially moved on to the next season's writers. Publishers love it when their writers win literary prizes and can usually be counted on to submit copies on your behalf.

Colonies and Retreats

Finally, this is the perfect time to attend an artist colony.

We've come full circle, since this book began with a description of my first colony experience, and ends with a discussion of colonies as well. But a colony or retreat is indeed a good way to "bookend" an experience. It allows you the time to really step back, relax, and consider your career as a whole.

Begin your colony search as you begin everything else — by going online and by perusing *Poets & Writers.* The turnaround time is long; most colonies require you to apply anywhere between six to eighteen months in advance, so if you want to attend a colony after your book is out, you'll need to apply before. Summers are the least likely time to be accepted, since that's often the only season when teachers are available to go to colonies, and they take a lot of the slots. If you're willing to visit Vermont in January, your chances improve. Also be aware that some — especially Yaddo and McDowell, which are the Yale and Harvard of colonies, and undeniable resume builders — are especially tough to crack. That doesn't mean that you shouldn't try, since it's a blind submission process with a rotating admissions panel. Newbies can get in and established writers can be rejected. But if you're inexperienced in the colony world, try several at once, including some of the smaller and lesser-knowns to increase your chances of getting accepted somewhere.

You'll apply for a certain season and request a certain amount of time — usually between two weeks and two months. In my opinion, two weeks is too short to get settled in and start real work and two months is so long that the colony begins to feel like real life, and thus you lose your focus. Three to five weeks is ideal. If you're accepted, they'll write back and offer you specific dates.

Why do I say that colonies are especially suitable for the post-pub letdown? Several reasons. One is that while conferences rev you up and get you focused — and thus are perfect for the time period when you're searching for an agent or getting ready to launch a book — colonies slow you down and help you get unfocused. You start to see the big picture again, to remember why you write, and you have the creative space to explore different ideas, determining which one you'd most like to develop.

They are also a tremendous balm for the soul. While publication rarely feels the way you thought it would feel, being in a colony almost always feels the way you expected. In fact, I would go so far as to say that colonies actually give you what you may have thought publication would — respect, assistance, the chance to commune with other artists, and large expanses of time alone with your thoughts.

Consider this story. Most of the time you have breakfast and dinner with the other colonists and lunch is delivered to your studio in a little basket or sack. This in itself is quite lovely, since they simply tiptoe up at some point in the middle of the day and you later open your door to find sandwiches and thermoses of soup and homemade cookies waiting. Great big portions to sustain you through an arduous afternoon of thinking, napping, and typing. Everyone gains weight at colonies. Everyone.

One day the sandwich was barbecue, which I love. Only the Southerner in me wanted to wash it down with some sweet tea, so after finishing my lunch I moseyed over to the kitchen in the main house to make some. The chef was in the kitchen already working on dinner when I entered, and she watched me zap a cup of water and a tea bag in the microwave, spoon in sugar, and pour the whole thing over ice. She remembered I was from North Carolina and asked if the barbecue was to my liking, and I said it was so great it had me craving sweet tea, just as all spicy food does.

Fast forward three weeks. The soup of the day was gazpacho, and sure enough, around 3 p.m. I needed my sweet tea fix. I walked over to the main house to find a fat glass pitcher — the kind in the Kool-Aid commercials — sitting on the dining table in a pool of sunlight. It had tea bags, sugar, and even a spiral-cut lemon floating in the water, and in front of it was a little hand-lettered sign that said "Kim." The chef told me that as she'd been packing the lunch baskets with the gazpacho she'd remembered I liked sweet tea with spicy food and had made a pitcher of sun tea just in case I showed up that afternoon.

Even now this story makes my chest tight. But that's the kind of gentle, individuated attention you get at a writing colony and why they're such a perfect place to hide and lick your post-publication wounds. These places exist not only to give you the time and space to pursue your writing but to constantly reassure you that writing is a worthwhile goal. If you're coming from the background of most writers — very little encouragement or support, families who want to know exactly when this strange little hobby of yours is going to start to pay off — the sight of a fat round pitcher of sun tea can reduce you to tears of gratitude.

So apply, and, if you get in, move heaven and earth to go. Accept that you may spend the first week unsettled, exhausted, and even weepy. Around week two the gears shift and you can start the kind of soul-deep work that's rarely possible in the jumble of home.

How the Second Book is Different

Writing your first book likely took forever. It's not uncommon to hear of writers spending five, ten, fifteen years on their debut fiction.

You may approach the second one differently. You're less willing to run down blind alleys, throwing away draft after draft before you eventually stumble on the best POV or the right structure. You're also now more aware of the village of people it takes to get a book launched, and how they can help or hinder your experience.

Now, what I'm about to say certainly isn't true for everyone. Some writers want nothing more than to leave the publication madness and return to their rooms, where they can once again immerse themselves in solitary work for as long as it takes. And that's great. Everyone has his own process.

But on the second time through, many of us opt to draw readers into the process earlier. Part of this is that published writers often have agents (and, if it's a multi-book deal, even editors) who are invested in our future work. Even more importantly, publication has helped us meet other writers and we're more likely than ever to have a strong circle of first readers who are qualified to give helpful feedback, even on rough and incomplete drafts.

The second book is a pivotal point and many writers stumble here. If you've developed sources of support through the process of publishing your first, consider using them to help make the second one easier. Note that I didn't say "easy." Writing a book is never easy, no matter how many you've done before, and I agree with Alison who, when asked, "What book is the hardest to write?" answered, "Whichever one you're working on at the time."

But if help is available, take it.

What it Takes for a Book — and an Author — to Make It

When I teach my MFA workshops, I'm often asked what's the most essential factor in making a book successful. Is quality writing enough in itself? Do you have to have a powerful story? Is it all about how hard the author and publisher work to sell the book? Is it a case of who you know? Or do some writers just manage to get lucky?

People are fiercely invested in the theories behind these questions. Some earnestly want to believe that a good book, like cream, will rise to the top no matter what. Others bitterly argue that publishing is a cynical business and it's all about kissing up to those above you on the ladder. Someone always thinks to mention the manically possessed author who spent years driving around the Midwest with copies of his book in the trunk of his car, practically bullying farmers into putting him on the best-seller list. Or what about that New Orleans-based book about floods that just happened to come out the week Katrina hit? And some cite writers who seem to succeed through a type of literary predestination, who are seemingly scooped up by the unseen hands of angels and placed on the highest clouds.

And then they ask me again what matters most: talent, story, connections, determination, or luck?

It would be nice if it only took any one of those things.

The truth is, to publish a successful book you need to have several factors on that list working in your favor. You don't have to have them all — everyone can name a badly written book that had a great hook of a story and just happened to hit the market at the right time, or a quiet little masterpiece of craft that somehow wound up in the hands of the most powerful agent in New York. But you have to have more than one of those things going for you or your book will sink.

Knowing this, it's smart to proceed on all fronts at once. Write the best book you can. Highlight the commercial elements of the story. Use every connection you have to draw attention to your work, be prepared to promote tirelessly, and don't hesitate to sacrifice a goat in your back yard the next time there's a full moon.

I'm serious about everything except possibly the goat.

And then get one other factor going in your favor as well. It's the one no one ever mentions, but it's a primary reason some writers develop ongoing careers while others founder. Develop professionalism, which means having the right attitude toward your work.

Look at it this way. A lot of people have talent. Many are born with it and MFAs are churning out more graduates each year, meaning that there are people who not only have raw talent but who have gotten instruction in how to hone it. The world is full of interesting stories. Plenty of people know people and plenty of people work hard, and I suppose you could even argue that a fair number of people manage to get lucky a fair amount of the time. But if you bring professionalism to your writing career — which is the sum total of all the things we've discussed in this book — you will have something rare.

Writing and publishing combine to create a strange and somewhat contradictory business. You have to be sensitive to do the job, but if you're too sensitive, the job will kill you. A large part of professionalism is developing a healthy detachment from certain aspects of publishing. Detachment doesn't mean you don't care. It's almost impossible to write a book without caring deeply. Detachment doesn't mean that you don't get involved with the promotional, financial, or marketing aspects of publishing. It's your responsibility to participate in every decision that you can. And detachment certainly doesn't mean that you take your hands off the steering wheel and let your book wind up wherever the fates take it. Being an author is a lot of hard work, including many chores you can't delegate to anyone else.

Instead, detachment means understanding where your efforts can make an impact and where they cannot. Certain factors are beyond your control. Let them go, and switch your focus to the areas where it will do you some good. And limit how much emotional energy you give to rejection, criticism, disappointment, and frustration.

Because, the reality is, the reason some writers thrive and others fail has more to do with attitude than talent.

On the surface, the math is discouraging. There are many more people out there who want to publish books than there are open slots at the publishing houses. But take into account that a lot of people vying for those slots self-eliminate. Imagine a horde of people thronging around before a marathon, all aimed toward the same finish line. Now imagine that just before the starting pistol goes off, ninety percent of those people bend down and tie their shoelaces together. Your odds of winning still aren't great, but they've just drastically improved.

The majority of writers make an already difficult challenge much harder than it has to be, simply because they don't approach publishing in a professional way. Agents, editors, and publicists pass them over in favor of people who understand this basic truth: that what it takes to write a book and what it takes to publish a book are two different things. Those who succeed learn how to navigate from the world of the writer to the world of the author and approach publishing with energy, practicality, resourcefulness, and an ego that's firmly in check. And if you learn to be both a writer and an author, this can be, without question, the most fulfilling job on the planet.

Helpful Websites for Authors

When Searching for an Agent

Scotteagan.blogspot.com — an agent who focuses on romance and women's fiction, but good info for anyone in an agent search.

Agentquery.com — a database of literary agents, info on how to write and submit a query, and how to avoid scams.

Pubrants.blogspot.com — an actually very nice agent politely rants about what drives her nuts, an insider's take on how not to query.

Queryshark.blogspot.com — how to revise bad query letters so that they work, the agent actually rewrites sub-par queries or points out where she would have stopped reading.

Querytracker.net — a list of 1200 + agents, also helps you organize and track your query letters to both agents and publishers.

Aaronline.org — Association of Authors Representatives info for your agent search, a list of member agents, all of whom must abide by a stated code of ethics.

General Publishing Info

Mediabistro.com — great source of media news, online classes, jobs in the industry.

Blog.nathanbransford.com — former agent turned YA writer, looks like a California surfer dude but gives great advice, his series of "publishing essential" posts worth their weight in gold.

Noveljourney.blogspot.com — features book reviews and writers discussing how they got their publishing start.

Pred-ed.com — general information but best known for pointing out scams.

Pimpmynovel.blogspot.com — a veteran of a publishing house sales department tells what happens to a book after it's acquired, funny, irreverent, not for the faint of heart.

E-publishing and Indies

Jakonrath.blogspot.com — outspoken proponent of indie publishing, full of tips on how to make it on your own.

Amandahocking.blogspot.com — indie publishing's most famous success story shares her insights.

Thewritersguidetoepublishing.com — answers to common e-publishing questions.

Bookcoverarchive.com — a roundup of book covers, a great starting place to what you might like and might not, especially helpful for indie authors and those working with small presses where their opinions might be sought.

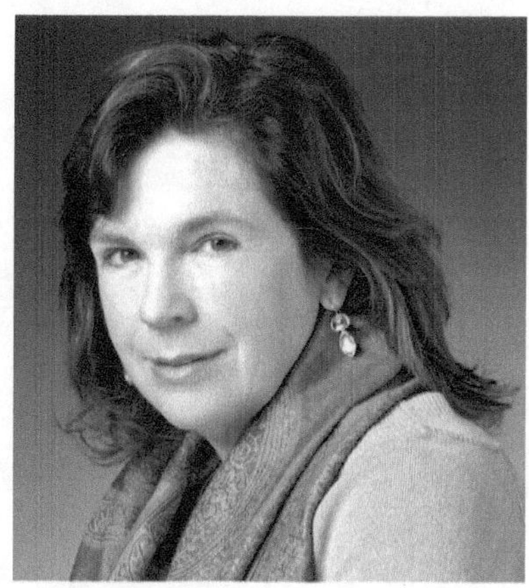

Kim Wright had been a full-time writer for thirty years, working primarily as a journalist specializing in food and wine. Her first novel, *Love in Mid Air*, was published by Grand Central in 2010, and she is presently working on a mystery about Jack the Ripper. She lives in Charlotte, NC with her dog/muse Otis, where she leads writing workshops in both the continuing education program and MFA program at Queens University. Her hobbies include ballroom dancing and travel.

www.ingramcontent.com/pod-product-compliance
Lightning Source LLC
LaVergne TN
LVHW091149080826
845145LV00008B/2307

* 9 7 8 1 9 3 5 7 0 8 4 2 1 *